Calling Arizona Home

FRED DUVAL

LISA SCHNEBLY HEIDINGER

Julie and Ed,

With warm regards
to the parents of one
of my favorite people.

Fred DuVal

Calling Arizona Home

FRED DUVAL

LISA SCHNEBLY HEIDINGER

ISBN: 0-9766340-6-6

Library of Congress Control Number: 2005930149

Published by:
Inkwell Productions
6962 E. First Avenue, Ste. 102
Scottsdale, AZ 85251
Phone: (480) 481-6036
Fax: (480) 481-6042
Toll Free: (888) 324-BOOK (2665)
Email: info@inkwellproductions.com
Web site: www.inkwellproductions.com

Cover & Interior design by Ronny Cromwell~ Graphix~Out West Today
Photography: Lisa Schnebly Heidinger

TABLE OF CONTENTS

Acknowledgments

While this book has been a life long aspiration, and a year long joy, no book can be written without the support of many people, and this effort is no different. First, I could not have enjoyed a better collaborator than Lisa Schnebly Heidinger. Lisa and I have known each other for 20 years, have been on opposite side of the political table (she a journalist, me a strategist), and have lived parallel lives. We both were raised in Tucson, lived in Flagstaff only to find ourselves each finally drawn to the opportunities of Phoenix. We have enjoyed many miles together over the past year during the creation of this book. Her love of Arizona equals mine, her gift of language exceeds mine, and she is good company – as such, the perfect partner for this project.

I am grateful to my parents Merlin DuVal and Carol DuVal Whiteman who rescued me from the soulless plains of Oklahoma and brought me to these rocks and rills and explored them with me in my youth. And who, I might add also introduced me to the joys of writing. Each – along with my step-father Jack Whiteman – has published their own texts and I suppose I have relished the chance to further the family tradition. To the rest of my family, Ruth, David, Barb, I offer my thanks for sharing your own love of our state. And in particular, I am grateful beyond words for Carol's and Barb's willingness to read the full text and make innumerable suggestions and improvements to it.

Many people played special roles in introducing the fullness of Arizona to me. Years ago a young geologist and historian named Bruce Babbitt and I drove back roads throughout the state. Bruce, who served as Arizona's Governor and as Secretary of the Interior under President Clinton, hailed from one of Arizona's pioneer families. His love of Arizona was infectious – and his knowledge always captivating. He had a strange but utterly charming habit on campaign trips of stopping at old cemeteries in small northern Arizona towns to catch up on who had passed on since his last visit, or perhaps to brush up on family trees for political context – I was never sure which – but the conversations that grew out of these detours left me with a deep interest in both. Years later as

Governor, with the benefit of the state plane, campaign trips became geology and history lessons from the sky. Bruce first took me to the Grand Canyon he so loves in the spring on 1974, and we have hiked, rafted and camped it each decade since. We will continue to do so as our limbs allow. These are truly gifts that keep on giving and which manifest in this text.

I have drawn inspiration from many distinguished and renowned authors that have helped me see more clearly that which was in front of me. These include historians Tom Sheridan and C.L Sonnichsen, authors of the West such as Gary Nabham, Rudolfo Anaya, Marshall Trimble and Wallace Stegner, and writers of "place" and community particularly including Scott Russell Sanders, Dan Shilling, Daniel Kemmis, and the Flagstaff Writers Group headed by my friend Jack Doggett.

I am grateful for the countless Arizonans who allowed us to meet and interview them. Their contributions to our state make it great and their stories are what have made this project such a joy.

I give thanks to publisher Nick Ligidakis, editor Cynthia Lukas, typesetter Ronny Cromwell, and the team of professionals at Inkwell Productions for their patience and professionalism, as well as their commitment to both a timely publication and a quality product.

And most importantly, to my wife Jennifer and my son Will I offer my deepest gratitude for your endless patience and support. More than any state, or city or place, it is with you that I am truly home. The many pages in this book contain my love for Arizona. Its length would be insufficient to contain my love for the two of you.

Fred DuVal
Flagstaff and Phoenix
January, 2005

Acknowledgments

When Fred invited me to co-author this book, I replied that I would love to participate; however, it would be his love letter to the state, rather than mine.

I didn't realize then that it is impossible for me to write about Arizona and not have it be a love letter, because to see any aspect of it is to fall in love all over again.

Traveling narrower roads than interstate, and gathering around tables with people who came and gave their time for no other reason than to help us understand their town has been a glorious honor. Residents in every geographic region of the state put aside other obligations and diversions to share their time with us, without ego or eagerness to be prominently mentioned. My only regret is not being able to include every quote.

But no one piece, be it one of Ed Mell's sweeping swaths of Grand Canyon captured on canvas, or Greg McNamee's poetic polemics on desert in prose, can include all that is Arizona. To do that may be a life's work, that can never be completed, for the face of the state changes at a rate more rapid than it can be definitively recorded for posterity. So this book is a collection of facets, not a three-dimensional model of the entire jewel.

What we've done is dip into various currents of the state's population. We've driven up corkscrew hills to look out over small downtowns, navigated rutted cemetery paths to get a sense of citizens gone before, and learned, at every turn, more about places we thought we already knew rather well. Then we wrote. After each draft, the first writer waited nervously while the other reviewed the pages, and sighed with relief each time the feedback was, "You said what I thought." All of this was done knowing it cannot be completely captured, but wanting so much to contribute to the body of work that hints at, points to, tries to explain Arizona.

First, I must thank Fred, for inviting me along on this ride, letting me share the fascination of the various coffee shops and the awe we felt walking away from people whose stories and hearts and characters could each easily be an entire book. For doing most of the driving on late night highways returning to our families. For giving me the opportunity to continue what Sharlot Hall set the standard for: illustrating Arizona through its people at a given point in time.

I owe much to the researchers and writers who published the books I rely upon to get things right: Bill Weir, Will C. Barnes, Larry Cheek and others. Also to my father, Larry Schnebly, for his patient and superhuman proofreading, as well as insightful guidance on my sometimes incomplete perceptions. (Mum, your blanket support is no less appreciated.) And, of course, again and always to my husband Tom, whose understanding of the urge to range and to report let me travel with minimal guilt, and whose faith in my writing ability has been the single biggest factor in any success I've achieved over the past 15 years. To my children, Sedona Lee and Rye Schnebly, I offer my love and hope that this book will work toward improving the magnificent state they joyously inhabit and enhance.

Lisa Schnebly Heidinger
New Years 2005

Preface

"Every stranger's face I see reminds me that I long to be,
Homeward Bound"

Simon & Garfunkel

Authors write books about what they know and what they love. So I suppose it was inevitable that mine would be about Arizona. But it is not really about a "state" – after all, Arizona is only political lines on a map – but rather it is about a "place". It is about the thousands of square miles of mountains and streams, the vistas and horizons. It is about the neighbors and neighborhoods, the history and the future we share. It is about our personal stories and why we are here, and what we have to preserve.

I fell in love with Arizona shortly after arriving in 1963. As a boy and in my teens, I explored Southern Arizona; I camped in the Catalina Mountains outside Tucson, fished in Patagonia, hiked in Arivaipa, and hunted in the White Mountains. High school competitions took me to Douglas, Sierra Vista, Globe and Yuma. Later I moved to Phoenix, from which I traveled to the central and northern parts of the state, explored the reservations, navigated the Colorado and hiked the northlands. While living in Flagstaff in 2000-02, I traveled virtually all the back roads of the high country, its canyons, and its vast open spaces. My life is deeply blessed by the friends I have made and kept from Page to Nogales and from Springerville to Yuma. So the seeds for this book have been planted throughout my life.

In my time in the White House I met with countless governors and mayors who were looking for various forms of federal assistance or regulatory restraint so that they could help their citizens build the communities they envisioned. I began to realize that people had a myriad of reasons for picking, and remaining in the communities they called home. At their best these visions were rooted in a shared sense of place, which in turn was rooted in its history, tradition, geographical location, and ultimately in the people they love and in lifestyles they prize.

If book writers have an "ah ha" moment, mine came when it was time to leave Washington D.C. following an eight-year assignment in the White House. I had traveled ample portions of the world and worked in dozens of other states. But when it came time to engage my family in a discussion of where we would live, we had a one-minute unanimous conversation to wit; "It is time to go home."

In many respects the history of Arizona was made by those in search; Spaniards searching for gold, Native-Americans searching for a safe place for sheep to graze, prospectors searching for valuable ores, growers searching for a stable water supply, tuberculars searching for cures, homebuyers searching for affordable housing, seniors searching for perfect leisure, and all too many throughout our history seeing the land of opportunity as a search for a quick buck.

After eight years away, returning home was a reawakening of the many things that we loved, as well as finding new things about our state that intrigued and captivated us. Our "discovery," then, is of Arizona the place and the people – and the relationship between the two. This book is an effort to tell that story. We hope to be cartographers of sorts, bringing to life through anecdote, story and observation the special places Arizonans call home.

Introduction

SEARCHING FOR ARIZONA

"If geography is destiny, Arizona was marked for greatness."
Anne Hodges Morgan in "Arizona Memories"

Arizona is just a state, in geographical and political terms. But it is so much more than that.

Places exist in their wilderness. Arizona includes its forests of high mountain conifer, pine and aspen; low mountain oak, juniper and pinon; mesas of desert mesquite, yucca, and creosote. Arizona is its rivers both wet and dry beds, its volcanic peaks and its ubiquitous granite and shale. It is the cold lushness of Alpine and the dry barren desert of Quartzsite.

Places exist in their names. Spanish names: Tumacocori, Arivaca, Casa Grande. Indian names: Coconino, Maricopa and Pima. The new-fangled names of our recent instant communities: Anthem, Sun City Grand and Agritopia. Some of our names commemorate pioneers: Williams, Douglas, Clifton and Sedona (named for the Great-Grandmother of the co-author), and a northern stretch of cities all were named after railroad executives including Kingman, Winslow, Holbrook and Seligman. Some tell stories: Bloody Basin, Show Low, Flagstaff and Why. And others notably don't: Snowflake has nothing to do with the weather, Mexican Water is dry and Copperopolis was an envisioned metropolis that didn't, well, metrop.

Most importantly, places exist in their people. A society's relationship to the environment around it is reciprocal: it both changes the physical world and is changed by it.

The subject of how people get along with each other and how they relate to the place they inhabit is as old as Aristotle's writings. It has been addressed in both the Old and New Testament, in Catholic social thought and by sociologists, political scientists and historians past and present. What we know for certain is that vibrant communities form around relationships and around special places of shared meaning and history.

Places can be defined by the type or nature of the people drawn to them such as the rugged and iconoclastic folks you find in Alaska, or the individualists of Key West. Each – in its own way – establishes the special connection we call "place."

The Arizona-based Navajo (Dine') tribal members were offered fertile agricultural land along the Arkansas River in Oklahoma but the Dine' chose to return to its 15,000 square miles of barren red clay country of the Four Corners region. It was after all – the place where the Dine' were created – having passed through three previous worlds to enter this one. That is a powerful sense of place. The interruption of those traditions and stories forever change the places where we live and how we live.

Cities, towns and other places are organic. They have a life force of their own. Their vital energy can be positive or negative. They can be healthy or sick, growing or dying. And our feelings about, and interaction with, these communities have profound implications for the direction they take. It is why this book examines Arizona communities.

We live in a time when our desire for community seems to grow in proportion to our sense that it is declining, or at least changing. Old notions of community, such as church suppers or gathering at the corner grocery store still sustain old smaller communities such as in St. Johns and Casa Grande. Longing for these forms of connection may explain in part why we see small town design features as part of the new urbanism in places like Anthem and Verrado. People in those towns spoke of the fear that globalization was robbing them of neighborhood connections, and that they missed the civility and inter-dependence of the communities of old. We are all reminded that, as Arizonan Susan Lamb writes in a collection of essays entitled, "The View

From Here, "No matter its size, a community forms slowly, quietly and from the heart, one relationship at a time".

All too often Arizonans refer to "home" as the place they have come from – even years after their move. Our own "Arizona Republic" has a weekly news column "News from Home," which subtly undermines our citizens' adoption of their new home state. For communities to thrive, its citizens must feel it is "home" and, as a result, assume a more meaningful commitment to its health, well-being and long term prosperity and survival.

To do that, we should examine who we are, where we came from, why we came, and how we keep these special places, well, special.

GRAND CANYON RAILROAD STATION

CHAPTER 1

MIGRATIONS: WHERE WE CAME FROM

"Eastward I go only by force; but westward I go free. The future lies that way to me, and the earth seems more unexhausted and richer there"
Henry David Thoreau in "Walden and Other Writings"

S ome of Arizona's earliest native citizens lived a stationary existence for more than ten thousand years. Oriabi, on the Hopi Third Mesa, is the longest continuously inhabited place in North America. But many Arizona Indians came here in search of good grazing land. Many others were forced to migrate here at the end of a cavalry pistol. A history of forced marches, forced off-reservation schooling, and the stories passed down from earlier native elders about these events, are a bitter introduction to our history.

The migration north from Mexico came in several major waves. The first migration occurred 350 years ago when the Spaniards traveled north in search of treasure and Christian converts. Coronado and others adventurers searching for the cities of gold were met with the disappointments of failure and the gorge of the impassable Grand Canyon. But that didn't stop the migration. However, a number of prominent Spaniards were given large land grants in Southern Arizona, which have left the borderlands rich with Spanish tradition and missions.

Today millions of Mexicans migrate north each year in search of greater prosperity. Many make it to Arizona and beyond for jobs in the northern and eastern United States. Cash has become the largest and fastest growing export from the states back into Mexico. Arizona's culture has been forever changed and enriched by those who came and stayed, and who brought with them the compelling strains of their native culture.

This migration pattern has changed, especially in the post 9/11 years. It seems that every year we read of more and more parched bodies of would-be migrants are found in the vast Arizona desert.

Every town in Arizona is touched by the border and many, such as Nogales, Douglas, South Tucson, Yuma, Globe, Hayden, Kearny, Eloy and others are living with two languages and two cultures. Diversity makes the challenge of building a shared state more difficult but it makes the rewards of doing so much richer.

Throughout our history the "West" has drawn migrants from the East of every social class and with every kind of ambition. Hundreds of thousands of ordinary people walked across this country, rode in wagons or on horse to settle in Arizona. They built ranches, farms, towns and cities.

Entrepreneurs like Edward Schieffelin (who struck the first ore in Tombstone and Bisbee), Walter Douglas (who served as both Chairman of Southern Pacific Railroad and President of Phelps Dodge), Michael Goldwater (a Jewish merchant who supplied consumer goods around the state) and the five Babbitt Brothers from Cincinnati (who started what became the largest cattle outfit in Arizona) have come west to invest and build legacies and fortunes.

The Chinese came to build the railroads and Hoover Dam, the Mexicans came to mine the gold and copper, and countless others came alone with hope of a lucky ore strike, to tend a few cattle, or to grow some crops and start anew. These pioneers were celebrated in history and lore for their pluck, grit and determination. And they started families and communities. They were Arizona's pioneers.

Among the most remarkable migrations was that initiated by Brigham Young in the 1870's. (The Navajos turned earlier Mormon migrations in the 1850's back). Having settled Salt Lake and built his church's governing temple there, he urged devout followers Jacob Hamblin and then William Flake to lead hundreds of his fellow Latter-day Saints to migrate south to settle the watershed of the Little Colorado River. Those pioneers built four early settlements, of which only Joseph City survives today.

One of the biggest hurtles to settling in Arizona was that the pioneers had to cross the raging Colorado River. (The Navajo say the Colorado has a female spirit named "Life Without End." She, and her male counterpart, the San Juan River, form a protective boundary around reservation lands.)

John D. Lee solved the problem of getting across the river by building a ferry to transport people, wagons and livestock. When traveling Mormon settlers arrived at the river, they rang a huge bell, called the "Lonely Bell". Lee then took them across the river. Lee's Ferry, as his homestead was known, was abandoned several years later, and the famous bell disappeared. (Years later it was discovered in the backyard of a Phoenix arts philanthropist.) But the ferry and bell had done their work and settlements successfully rooted in Holbrook, Winslow, Snowflake, Taylor, Show Low, St. Johns and Springerville.

In 1877 another group of Saints left St. George, Utah to settle the Salt River Valley, and started Lehi, which is known today as Mesa. In 1885 Mormons made up 11 percent of the state's population – a figure that has remained consistent through the last hundred years.

The fortitude of these early migrants and settlers, the Native-Americans, Mexicans, Cowboys, Farmers, and Mormons, have left an indelible mark on the nature of the place we call Arizona. The harder the country, the more fiercely it selects its inhabitants because it repels those not willing to pay the price. The "rugged individualist" ethic is found to this day in the ambition of Arizona businesspeople and in those still striking out on new ventures.

Modern day migrants also include those who have chosen to serve their country in the military. They have come in droves to Arizona's open landscape, reliable weather and supportive politics. In 1941 Luke Air Force Base was started on 1,440 acres near Glendale and became the largest advanced flying school in the world, generating millions a year for local business. Soon thereafter, promoted by Arizona's venerable Senator Carl Hayden and aided by year-round flying weather, Arizona landed Williams Field near Chandler, Thunderbird, Litchfield Naval Air Facility, Davis-Monthan near Tucson (which has the world's largest supply of plane parts in the world), Ryan Field, Marana Air Base, and Fort Huachuca near Sierra Vista.

The Army made many similar if smaller investments. The soldiers came – and stayed. Civilians soon followed, building Goodyear Aircraft Corp (which grew to 7,500 employees – once the largest employer in the Valley), Alcoa, Sperry-Rand, AiResearch, Motorola and others. The military migration was enormous from the 1940's to the present day, and the impact on Arizona's economy, politics and civic life has been significant.

The largest migration in recent time is seniors searching for the perfect retirement. The establishment of the first Sun City in 1962 put Del Webb on the cover of Time magazine, and started a boom that has put tens of thousands of seniors in manicured, fully contained retirement communities around the state, and predominately on the northwest side of Phoenix. This brand new sense of "place." was completely man-made and artificial in a sense, but it has been widely successful for the lifestyle it guaranties its residents. It has also, incorrectly, given Arizona the image of being populated disproportionably by seniors. Arizona actually has the same number of young residents as it does seniors. Nevertheless, these communities have forever changed Arizona's sense of place.

Then there is the "snowbird" population. Every autumn brings many thousands of winter visitors who are escaping the snowdrifts and artic chills of their home states for a few weeks or months. Cactus League baseball also brings a multitude of fans here during the spring and each fall many thousands of new college students arrive to attend one of our three fine State Universities.

Many from all of these groups find the sun, lifestyle and opportunities worth staying for on a permanent basis.

Some of our newest residents are seeking a quieter life in the rural parts of Arizona. For them, history has come full circle. Communities, which were vibrant in early days of pioneering Arizona, have been rediscovered for their histories and their climates. Prescott, Bisbee, and Flagstaff are being embraced for their authenticity. Others, like Payson, Cottonwood, and Sierra Vista, are being rediscovered for their perfect climates. These new residents – unlike the migrant waves before them – share no ethnicity, occupation or age in common. They seek only a better life.

While we have huge waves of people moving to Arizona, we also have many people moving away. Arizona is the second fastest growing state in the nation, and the third with the most transients. The average residency is 6 years, and for every three arrivals into Arizona, two migrate out.

Some communities suffer from isolation. Native American tribal members with their unique cultural dynamics, who generally have great distances between communities, remain largely on their reservations. Mexican migrants frequently lack both mobility and English-speaking skills. Because they fear discrimination and deeply prize the proximity of blood relations they generally stay in Spanish-speaking enclaves. And even in residential areas of our cities and towns, gated communities, seeking exclusivity or homogeneity, pose their own obvious barriers to community.

So who are we? We are native Indians, cowboys and farmers, Hispanics and Mormons, military and high-tech professionals, families, kids, seniors and university students – most at one time or another from someplace else. While the stories of our individual lives differ, the story of our respective migrations is similar. We are here because we saw and followed opportunity. Newcomers shuck their old ties and traditions as the new lifestyle of the "great open" ignites their ambitions. And we get to live in a glorious setting.

That is the kind of place Arizona is.

Arizona offers the most versatile piece of Mother Nature's handiwork in North America. In it's diversity of geography it is blessed with the windswept sands of the Mohave Desert and the moist green meadows of the White Mountains, by the stark drama of the saguaro silhouetted against the cragged rock mountains and mile after mile of fertile soil. Arizona has built the newest large city in America, and celebrates some of the oldest.

That is the kind of place Arizona is.

It is **Prescott**. Arizona's first capital. Prescott celebrates local traditions that would be the envy of any city of the original American colonies.

It is **Casa Grande**. A growing city that enjoys the most positive civic spirit in the state. Casa Grande has an optimism that is contagious.

It is **Sedona**. A place of rare light and singular beauty, Sedona's future will require the individualists who are drawn there, to cooperatively protect the unique environment from threatening rapid development.

It is **St Johns.** A town with wide, quiet streets, settled peacefully by Mormons and Mexicans, it has grown little over the years. St Johns celebrates a tradition that for high school graduates who leave, one returns home to take his or her place.

It is **Flagstaff**. A small city steeped in old history and new traditions such as its charming Farmers Market, "Flag" has all the necessary assets for a big future. But it faces economic challenges of equal proportion.

It is **Sun City**. The model that paved the way for imitations across Arizona and the nation, Sun City nurtures the youth in everyone, no matter how old.

It is **Sierra Vista.** A town that is growing exponentially in size and in pride, Sierra Vista is brimming with civic activity, and enjoys a relationship with neighboring Fort Huachuca that would be a model for any military town.

It is **Holbrook**. Born of Mormon roots and sustained by earlier generations of tourists who now skip this stop on the Interstate, while Holbrook appears to currently enjoy more history than future, it also has an unsurpassed civic commitment.

It is **Douglas.** This charming copper town's future is uniquely linked to Mexico and the daily economic and personal interchange that crosses the border, both ways, every day.

It is **Kingman.** While once a major way station on Route 66 facing stagnation. Kingman has begun to effectively leverage its airport, reinventing itself into one of the fastest growing small towns in Northern Arizona.

It is **Tucson.** Under Mexico's rule till 1864, it emerged to become the former Territorial capitol and Arizona's largest city until 1920. Tucson springs from an ancient presidio and the banks of the Santa Cruz, and celebrates this heritage as it grows into a major American city.

It is **Globe-Miami**. These two cities endured generations of spirited competition on the football field only to recently forge bonds of interdependence focused on a future beyond copper.

It is growth towns that were some developer's vision of a perfect life – that got it right. **Lake Havasu City** on the banks of the Colorado, **Anthem** and **Verrado** create urban amenities without the urban, and even **Quartzsite** grows in the cool season to tens of thousands of visitors who just as quickly move on as the temperature rises.

It is **Phoenix.** Known to the rest of the state as the "State of Maricopa," the Phoenix metropolitan area is the economic lifeblood of Arizona. Yet it struggles to create an identity that unites and bonds its residents.

In every city and town across the full sweep of an enormous state we find a consistent and relentless optimism. Limitless and open vistas seem to encourage a more expansive and hopeful attitude.

That is the kind of place Arizona is.

GLOBE ARTS CENTER

CHAPTER 2

EXTRACTION BOUNTIES: WHY WE CAME

"Wherever there was a rumor and a hole in the ground,
someone built a town around it."

Mark Twain said of Arizona.

People migrated because Arizona offered something to everyone.

Arizona's fertile soil has been called upon to help feed the nation, and our farmers have responded with some of the most bountiful harvests anywhere. Along with cattle, climate and copper, Arizona's 5 "C's" of economic growth included citrus and cotton. Many different crops were grown in this critical industry, but citrus and cotton have been its main staples. Towns like Safford, Casa Grande and Yuma remain linchpins in the growers' community and the agricultural industry.

Today, the world our farmers face is far different from earlier years. New complicated laws on price supports, international trade, and most importantly, on water usage require as much business acumen as hard work to survive. Tired of being stretched between business and farming, many are quitting. Some are also being pushed out by the spreading urbanization that consumes an acre an hour of Arizona's agricultural land. This change slowly extinguishes a revered lifestyle. Once agricultural towns like Buckeye, Casa Grande and Chandler are slowly losing the battle to dense housing and urban development.

At one time, copper was the king of Arizona's economy and politics by generating tens of million of dollars of value (ten-fold that number in today's dollars.) It was an enormous contributor to the world's supply of ore – and supplied half of our own nation's demand. Arizona copper was once the most pure and valuable of any produced in the world. Phelps Dodge copper supplied the wire for America's first transcontinental telephone lines. Thousands came to mine it, and hundreds died doing so. At the turn of the century one in five Arizona men were in mining-related work. Bitter battles waged over it as labor strikes split households. In one tragic instance, Arizona copper miners on strike in Bisbee were loaded on padlocked boxcars and literally railroaded out of Arizona.

All too often, absentee landlords made their great profits off the backs of Arizona miners and moved on. Phelps Dodge was headquartered in New York City, Shannon Consolidated in Boston, Arizona Copper in Edinburgh, Scotland. The New York Guggenheims controlled the Kennecott and Ray mines while the Lewisohms controlled Miami. Arizona became known as a rental state. Towns like Jerome, Globe, Hayden, San Manuel, Kearny, Douglas, Bisbee, and Clifton-Morenci were born on the fortunes of copper – and many were extinguished with those fortunes, as well. Copper, like gold and silver before it, was an unsustainable extraction, leaving a scarred earth and broken communities behind.

Nothing in Arizona history has been more powerful, more productive, greedier and more divisive than King Copper. Fortunately, more enlightened leadership has taken the helm of Arizona copper and seeks to sustain production in the face of lower cost overseas competitors – while improving employee relations.

If Southern and Eastern Arizona sacrificed its ore, Northern Arizona gave up its forests. When the Santa Fe railroad sliced across Northern Arizona in 1880, it paralleled the largest stand of Ponderosa Pine in the continental United States. Because those forests sat on flat plateaus rather than mountainsides, they were easily accessible (and therefore very profitable to absentee lumbermen such as Edward Ayers of Chicago and William Cady of Louisiana). But the forestry industry, unlike the copper extraction, often included Arizona-based companies. The venerable Riordan family bought the Ayers operation, and Thomas Pollock of Flagstaff developed the first logging operation on the Apache Reservation. While this produced slightly more responsible asset management, as with any finite resource, it met the same ultimate result. Arizona was once the fourth largest producer of lumber, and its largest operation, Southwest Forest Inc., briefly entered the Fortune 500 list. Today virtually all of Arizona's forest operations have shut down, inevitably leaving a diminished resource, fallow and forgotten mills, and devastated families in its wake.

The cattle industry has also suffered its share of booms and busts. It started with small herds owned by Arizona families such as the Eliases in Southern Arizona, the Redondos in Yuma, and small ranchers near Prescott and Wickenburg like the Middletons and the Ellisons. But the 1877 Desert Land Act, which quadrupled homestead allotments, spurred a cattle boom in the 1880's. The game was on for the onslaught of big and often out-of-state-business. General Henry Hooker of the Sierra Bonita Ranch and Colin Cameron of Pennsylvania who started the San Rafael Cattle Company were sophisticates who had not only access to eastern financial backers, but also visions as large as the range. At one time over one million sheep and one million cattle fed off Arizona soil. But greed led too few ranchers to limit their herds, and before long a confluence of overgrazing and drought in the early 1890's cost the industry severely. In Southern Arizona well over half the stock perished from starvation and thirst.

With range management and thoughtful self-governance, the industry managed to rebound and survive over the past hundred years. While no longer the fourth largest producer of beef in the United States as in the earlier days of the enormous "Hashknife" outfit of the Aztec Land and Cattle Company, the Empire and Wingfield Ranches and the CO Bar, many Arizonans are still able to make a living raising cattle. But as with agriculture, it is an increasingly challenging way of life as the pressures of international trade and governmental dictates complicate the business.

The next Arizona commodity ripe for exploitation was sunshine. The promise of unlimited land at cheap prices has made real estate sprawl the dominant industry in the modern era. Arizona has hosted the largest land rush since Oklahoma making it possible for millions to move here and prosper. Phoenix has grown into the sixth largest city in the United States, and the surrounding suburbs combined, double its population. Earlier waves of growth were fueled by the completion of the railroad, by tuberculars seeking dry heat, by the invention of the swamp cooler, the arrival of enormous military installations, and most recently the promise of "new economy" jobs or a perfect retirement. But underlying all of it was the promise of cheap housing and steady sunshine. That promise is now gone. While construction and tourism remain two of the most stable sectors in Arizona's economy, the price of housing skyrocketed in the early 21st century, pushing prices dramatically upwards and sending development sprawl further and further away from the urban centers.

Growth has become an economic addiction, creating enormous wealth and a plethora of opportunity. But taking from the lessons we've learned from earlier booms and busts, what are the limits to growth? In our indigenous western optimism and vision, we have created a lifestyle seemingly devoid of limits. We have conquered the desert with air conditioning and water reclamation projects and have built a false oasis of man-made lakes, golf courses and swimming pools.

This brings us to the crossroads Arizonans are facing today. We have built an economy and a lifestyle based upon it. Arizona has been consumed. As we grow toward 10 million residents in the next decade, how will we live differently in our place? Will we align ourselves to the grain of our place and time – and respond to its needs?

The Historian Tom Sheridan writes in his definitive "Arizona: A History:" "If we want to create a society in Arizona that is more than a series of booms and busts, we need to make the fit between nature and culture more like a membrane and less like a life support system."

The Navajo have a fundamental belief that when you take something from the earth you must give something back. It is a tradition worth emulating. When a decision is made, the question that should be asked is, "How will this affect future generations?" How do we all become natives of this place we call home?

LEE'S FERRY ORCHARD

SAN XAVIER TOWERS

CHAPTER 3

WHO WE ARE NOT: WESTERN MYTHS

"There is something about exposure to that big country that not only tells an individual how small he is, but steadily tells him who he is."
Wallace Stegner

Gary Cooper, the solitary, stoic and honor-bound marshal, standing alone at high noon on the dusty street of town, facing the outlaws with only his colt and his badge, is the essence of the American image of the West. The prevalence of myths about westerners is almost overwhelming. We easily succumb to the marketing appeal to define who we are – self-reliant individualists battling the bad guys, the cowardly townspeople, the scorpions and snakes to make our community secure. Or, in the whip-lashing world of modern marketing, we are shown Arizona as filled with golf-cart riding seniors living in "retirement communities" that are devoid of urban centers or young people.

Without question a spirit of independence and self-reliance has always been plentiful in Arizona. Early settlers demonstrated fortitude and resilience in staking their futures in a barren, hot, unpopulated and often lawless Arizona. Arizona grew and prospered on the wallets of risk-taking entrepreneurs and on the backs of cheap immigrant labor. Cowboys and farmers arrived alone and with little to their name but hopes for their future.

This independent pioneer attitude is still with us today. Arizona is a leader in new business starts, creative government and the arts. We are hospitable and open to anyone with ambition, ideas, or simply a devoted work ethic. We often live life on the edge, as illustrated by both our record number of business starts and a commensurate number of bankruptcies. The character of the old Wild West is still prevalent in our more recent history of quick buck artists and insufficiently regulated savings and loans.

We rightfully celebrate and cherish the notion of western independence and rugged individualism, with "Wild West" cowboy archetypes and anti-government diatribes. "Leave us alone" is a feel-good rally cry for some politicians, business people and landowners.

The truth is, in the 21st Century, none of us can live by our wits or courage alone – and we never could. (Even Gary Cooper got emotional support when his pacifist bride Grace Kelly stands by him.) For even the barest of existence we depend on the labors of other people, the fruits of the earth, and the inherited benefits of our place. Indian communities relied on everyone's help to channel water for crops. Early settlers relied on neighbors to raise a roof. Farmers needed pickers, markets and systems of distribution to sell their produce. Later they needed price supports to protect against seasonal losses. Cattlemen turned to law enforcement to protect against rustlers, as did prospectors to protect their claims.

Myth 1. We are a State of Seniors.

The Sun Belt image of Arizona being a Mecca for senior migration is entirely true, but it masks the full reality that the growth in our senior population is dwarfed by other in-migration. Young families with children make up a large portion of our population and in fact, Arizona has a slightly disproportionate percentage of both seniors and children, and notably a much higher average of young families than most states.

This disproportion of population ages is responsible for one of our biggest political headaches – the battles between those who – having already educated their children – oppose greater taxation for social investments in education and welfare, and those who most need those investments.

Myth 2: We are a Rural State.

The second prevailing myth is that Arizona is a rural state. Arizona Highways magazine cleverly reinforces the popular Eastern image of our vast wide-open spaces with each Arizonan enjoying their sunset from a long veranda spanning across the open unobstructed plain.

And of course, that image is far from reality.

We are one of the most urban states in the United States, with 80 percent of our growing population living in one of two large urban areas (Phoenix and Tucson), with over 60 percent of that number in just one of them.

Issues that defined our development in the past such as land use, agricultural policy, forest policy, rural highways and the like, now take a back seat to the pressing problems facing any fast-growing urban area. These include urban water use, the protection of open space, crime, and transportation. The transition from a rural to an urban state over the past century has eroded some Arizona tradition and has created a very uneven appreciation of history.

Myth 3: Our relationship to the federal government.

But the biggest myth has to do with our western relationship to government. Our state hobby is to scorn it – particularly the "feds" in Washington. The reality is that if the federal government had "left us alone" there would be no Arizona, as we know it. Like it or not, Arizona has a very close relationship with government – particularly the federal government. It has always, and continues to, play an integral part in defining Arizona and its people.

- Over 70 percent of Arizona is in some way controlled by the federal government. This includes tribal land, military bases, forestland, National Parks and land managed by the Bureau of Land Management for multiple uses.

•   The federal government negotiated treaties with the Native tribes and opened the door to incoming Anglo settlers.

•   Federal contracts – often granted without competitive bidding – assured profitable yields for some of Arizona's largest logging businesses.

•   Federal initiatives opened up international markets for Arizona silver and copper.

•   The completion of the inter-continental railroad, facilitated by federal dollars, initiated one of Arizona's economic booms and made it possible for our cattle and agricultural producers to get goods to market.

•   The New Deal was a bonanza for Arizona. Twenty-seven percent of Arizonians, one of the largest percentages in the nation, received welfare; we had more Conservation Corps assistance (28 camps) than most states; the federal price supports for cotton and other agricultural goods protected Arizona's largest growers from unstable prices; the WPA employed over 16,000 Arizonans and built over 163 public buildings and facilities; ranching legislation protected large cattle ranchers with tariff barriers; the "feds" built Hoover Dam and employed almost 5,000 people doing it; and the Federal Housing Act provided affordable housing for thousands of new Arizona workers.

•   By the end of the New Deal, the federal government had spent three times the per capita national average in Arizona. Historian Lawrence Arlington estimates that Arizona received about $342 million in federal assistance between 1933 and 1939 – while paying in about $16 million in federal taxes.

- Hundreds of millions of dollars of Pentagon funds have created thousands of high-paying jobs on Arizona Bases, and also stimulated valuable private economic activity in nearby cities. To this day, enormous Pentagon contracts make it possible for thousands of Arizonans to work on missiles, helicopters and a myriad of technology manufacturing.

- The role of the federal government in water management has been paramount and indispensable to our growth and development. The building of the Roosevelt Dam and creation of the Salt River Project was an unprecedented federal commitment dwarfed only by the grand-daddy of all federal assistance – the Central Arizona Project. The CAP, which brings Colorado River water to Arizona's urban areas, is the nation's biggest reclamation project. Without it, our agricultural sector would wither and our steady real estate-based economy would dry up like the sand on which it is built.

- Though the federal government's treatment of, and interactions with, Arizona's tribes has been seldom altruistic and often shamefully unjust, the importance of federal dollars to the state's Indian tribes is indisputable.

- In the 1980's, Arizona's own Lincoln Savings and Loan was the largest thrift failure in the United States, costing taxpayers over 3 billion dollars. And Arizona banks – too eager to get in on real estate speculation – lost more federally insured money than any other banks in the country.

- And in 2005, a federal commitment of hundreds of millions of dollars will enable Phoenix to build a light rail system to unclog its major arterial roads and freeways.

In all of these cases of agricultural support, logging contracts, military offshoots, and banking bailouts, the ironic beneficiaries of federal largess are the very industry and big business communities that most demonstrably scorn the federal role and hug the mythological western ethic of the rugged individualist.

Del Webb is a particularly good example. Webb made a fortune on New Deal-funded homes and government office construction, then captured the contracts to build every major military base in Arizona (save for Davis-Monthan). In the Cold War period Webb built veterans hospitals and missile silos, and following the federal construction of the CAP that assured a water supply, built enormous retirement communities. Yet, in his later years, Webb became a vocal political champion of the conservative anti-government cause!

The Forest Service, the National Parks Service, the Bureau of Land Management, the Bureau of Indian Affairs, the Department of Defense and countless other federal agencies are often irritating nuisances and often deserving of vociferous criticism. They are often smug, arrogant and ignorant. But their existence and ours has always been interdependent. To pretend we have built this oasis in the desert without them is to live a myth.

EMPIRE RANCH

SEDONA HALF DOME

CHAPTER 4

SO, WHO ARE WE?

"I shall never be able to tell you the grandeur of these mountains
nor the glory of the color that wraps the burning sands at their feet.
We shoot arrows at the sun in vain: yet we still shoot."
John Van Dyke, An early Arizona essayist, "The Desert" in 1903

We are a largely urban-based state with relatively new residents and an average age distribution. And we enjoy an unusually high reliance on the federal government as a partner in our growth and development. We are individualists who depend on each other.

We have a long history. While we have an image of ourselves as pioneers of the "Wild West," our legacy boasts of the ancient Salt River Hohokam which left indications of being one of the most advanced societies in North America at that time.

Rural Arizonans have visible history to bank on. Prescott, Globe, Tucson, Douglas, Bisbee, Holbrook, Flagstaff, and other cities and towns, honor their history and from it create a sense of community that is a cushion against economic misfortune and change, and is the key to civic pride and an enduring spirit.

The towns of Nogales, South Tucson, Eloy, Hayden, Globe and others share a link as a corridor of northern Mexican migration that has left each with intermarriages, shared families, holidays, cultural traditions and a common identification with Mexican culture.

Similarly, the historical flow of Mormons from Utah has left the towns of Holbrook, Heber, St Johns, Snowflake, Safford and Mesa with a rich genealogical history and common identity.

The Route 66 cities of Kingman, Seligman, Flagstaff, Winslow and Holbrook share a piece of national nostalgia as each moves in its own way beyond its dependency on the Mother lode of the former Route 66 "Mother Road."

The Colorado River cities of Bullhead City, Lake Havasu City, Parker and Yuma share a destiny tied to the river that flows by their front door and sustains their existence.

Newer Arizona has different challenges. Places like Anthem, Sun City, Sedona, Lake Havasu City and Sierra Vista are finding innovative ways to build community that are creating new traditions. Sedona is becoming a magnet for the arts and music, while Anthem has initiated a number of annual athletic competitions that draw from throughout the region. Clubs and civic groups are organizing around contemporary interests, while the same church traditions that provided community building to early settlers maintain their importance and relevance today. Phoenix and Tucson have become large cities with major centers for the arts and education, but struggle with the negative impacts of rapid growth.

Arizona is a state of vast differences in its land and its people. It is also a place of community, deep caring for its natural wonders, and common bonds that are moving us into the future.

BISBEE

Tucson Catalinas

CHAPTER 5

TUCSON: THE NEW OLD PUEBLO

For 12,000 years people have lived in this lovely Sonoran Desert basin surrounded by mountain ranges. Tucson is a relatively "wet" desert, with about eleven inches of rainfall per year, giving it a lushness not usually found in deserts. In fact, Tucson's name reflects its geography and meteorology. It comes from the Pima words "Chuk Son," meaning "spring at foot of black mountain."

In 1776, the improbably named Spanish emissary Hugo O'Connor established the Presidio de San Augustin to protect nervous settlers from Native American uprisings, and Tucson became America's first walled city. Bits of the presidio wall can still be seen downtown.

The frontier town went through an unattractive adolescence, booming to about 7,000 people in 1800. For the next century Tucson was known for the boozing, brawling and shooting that erupted in the dusty streets helping to put the "wild" in the "west." The fun didn't last.

Tucson was part of Mexico, but the United States coveted the Mexican lands and declared war to assert ownership. Mexico lost, giving California, New Mexico, Texas and most of Arizona, to the U.S. in 1848. Unfortunately that didn't include Tucson, which still belonged to Mexico.

Problems rose because the Mormon Battalion (which came to fight in the Mexican War) had settled in Tucson and refused to leave. Mexico tried for years to evict them, but gave up in 1854 when it helped get itself out of debt by selling 30,000 square miles of southern Arizona to the U.S.

Tucson suffered in ignominy of being captured by Rebel troops during the Civil War. The troops weren't in occupation for too long before Union soldiers evicted them after the battle of Picacho Peak – the Civil War's westernmost battle.

Families, ranchers and farmers began arriving on the Butterfield Stage Coaches. These citizens steadily built a real community in Tucson, fondly calling it "The Old Pueblo." Anglo men came west and intermarried with Mexican and Indian women. A scattering of Chinese railroad workers settled and opened businesses. A few former slaves settled in Tucson, but it was so far out in the Sonoran Desert and news traveled so slowly that news of the Emancipation Proclamation didn't reach Tucson until two years after it was signed!

Tucson had a spot of brief glory when it captured the state capital for about 10 years, before relinquishing to Phoenix.

By the 1950's, Tucson had become a bucolic pueblo of about 50,000 souls, mostly an amalgamation of Anglo and Hispanic. (Interestingly, this population mix has remained steady for the past 100 years. In 2000, Tucson was 35 percent Hispanic, 54 percent Anglo, 2.5 percent Asian and 2.5 percent African American.) But Tucson was beginning to grow up. New neighborhoods extended as far east as a dirt road named "Wilmot" after an early citizen. Women dressed up to go downtown; the barrio was rich with family history and neighborhoods exuded local culture.

Then, almost overnight, Tucson began to sprawl in huge leaps. "Progress" beat tradition at the polls every time. The elegant Spanish-style El Conquistador Hotel was razed to the ground. In its place, a new mall named the El Con was built. Only a nearby water tower echoing El Conquistador's grand architecture remains, a sentry of a forgotten age.

When community leaders observed that while still a vibrant place, the downtown barrio was getting shabby, Tucson removed a portion of it and on that land built an expensive new community center. Barrio Historico and other neighborhoods became elegiac names on the rosary beads of a lost heritage.

Even so, Tucson knew who she was. Her landmarks included the Tia Elena Restaurant on Grant Road with its surreal sculpture of almost anime design 40 years ahead of its time. The Arizona Inn still welcomed wealthy winter visitors from the east to its lovingly maintained grounds and gracious library. The University of Arizona Wildcat fans had tailgate parties, and cheered, or mourned their football team and cursed their coach, while basketball tickets were coins of the realm. Students drove by their headlights up "A" Mountain, or out to Gates Pass for a little romance.

Some of these things are still true. But today Tucson is swelling at the seams, annexing land and swelling again. Unlike many places however, Tucsonans don't really want to continue to grow, and never really did. "We used to be a little one-horse town," says Ron Caviglia, a longtime local developer. "Now, we're a big one-horse town." Broadcast veteran Jack Jacobson agrees. "Tucson will always retain a small-town atmosphere, no matter how big it gets."

In Tucson, residents seem to make repeated pilgrimages to the places that define the Old Pueblo. The list of special places shifts with the list-maker, but many would include Ted DeGrazia's Gallery of the Sun at Swan and Skyline, with its tobacco cans and whimsical figures added to the decor that makes it still fresh and puzzling; El Torrero, with its oddly lit walls and succulent handmade tortillas; the neighborhood of El Encanto, with homes built by old magnates now being restored to their older charm; the Cushing Street Bar and Grill still flourishing in one of the old barrio homes that survived urban renewal.

Many Tucsonans love to climb the trail up Sabino Canyon, with its bridges slippery from snowmelt in the winter and spanning a cool stream of water in the summer. Others take pleasure in leaving work early for baseball's Spring Training at Hi Corbett Field.

A trip to Saguaro National Monuments East and West fills the eye with desert splendor. "I came from Minnesota when I was 14, and fell in love with the Sonoran desert," says Paul Eckerstrom, a local attorney. "This was a totally different place; everything was brown but bright." He remembers his first look at Gates Pass. As a teenager he explored the land, the ghost towns, the vestiges of territorial Tucson, and still marvels how time can fall away. "It's like in Tucson, you aren't necessarily even in the present," he says. A strong environmental lobby keeps an eye on growth versus open space. Most Tucsonans were pleased when community and Congressional leadership expanded the Monument's area.

Chris Helms has been steeped in Sonoran desert and environmental issues throughout his career and says the Sonoran desert "is part of what I'm about." A quarter century on the city's west side has given him a deep reverence for the land and the people who inhabit it. "We have the best Hispanic-Anglo relations of any place I know," he says.

Tucsonans buy strings of fragrant chilis from street-corner vendors, replace winter rye on front lawns with sage and lantana, and actually show up at zoning meetings to retain the Sonoran character of the town. Any Tucsonan will tell you that people move to Tucson for the lifestyle. Dean Smith, a genial union and political activist says, "I'm not fond of cactus. But what holds me to Tucson is the melting pot. I love the mix of people you run into. Most aren't from Arizona, but everyone is part of it now."

The challenge facing Tucson today is keeping the lifestyle while new enthusiasts move here in record numbers. Traffic presents one of the biggest challenges. Unlike the neighboring metropolis of Phoenix to the north, Tucson has resisted freeways and parkways.

"Tucson's growth shows up in the traffic," says retired broadcast executive George Wallace, shaking his head. "The city fathers have not taken care of that. And they probably never will." Part of that is the residents' reluctance to finance road projects. "I always blame the new people who have moved to Tucson and don't want to spend tax money," says Wallace. "I'm not sure I can prove that. "But," he adds, echoing the reluctance to get into freeways: "We don't want to be like Phoenix."

Tucson compares itself to Phoenix the way San Diego does to Los Angeles, a state away. Also smaller and farther south, the city claims to have retained its character while the behemoth to the north sold its soul for a mess of people. "The Great State of Maricopa" is the older sibling no one here wants, while Pima County residents jealously watch the power and money coagulate in Phoenix.

Art Waller, listening, agrees. "Maricopa County does things Pima County wouldn't. In Pima County, you throw an issue in the air and about 80 different groups fire at it. As a consequence, very little gets done here." But before the discussion slides into a round of "Ain't it awful," Scott Vaughan speaks up. "I came here to go to the U of A, lived here 22 years, left for 10 and came back," he says. "Tucson has natural attributes that transcend economic issues. Here, we adjust cheerfully to hard times, and that's a key to continuing. You get to feel so welcome; I think people weather the problems because of the happiness here."

He agrees traffic is a challenge. "People will always find something to bitch about. You can worry about it, if you want to change the world. I just want to live the rest of my life in comfort and joy."

That illustrates another challenge for Tucson; it may be mired in too much well-intentioned debate. It often feels crippled by painful introspection caused by "growth schizophrenia." Most residents would say that's preferable to acting rashly and regretting it. But like Flagstaff, Tucson is not hampered by apathy. Active groups of protestors and petition-passers become galvanized about issues from new neighborhoods to social services.

Brian Flagg, a young man with no Old Pueblo pedigree, became a bugler for the rights of the Tucson homeless back in the early 80's, and tirelessly sounded the alarm until churches and civic groups gradually realized they were needed. Today, parishes and community groups still respond to many of the needs of the homeless.

It's been twenty years since Reverend John Fife made national news for leading the Sanctuary movement, helping to hide and transport refugees from Nicaragua and other places to the south. He and his followers were tried in federal court for their efforts. No one ended up in prison, but his final sermon before his sentencing about sometimes facing "roads down which you would rather not go" in order to serve your fellow man captured a flavor of Tucson. People give quietly.

The Tucson community showed its civic pride when it rallied and won the medical school for the University of Arizona. The founding dean, Dr. Merlin DuVal, tells of the remarkable community support during the fight. He tells the story about the guys at the local gas station who pooled their tips to help fund the medical school and turned them over to him every time the Dean filled up his car. And there were the hundreds of five- and ten-dollar donation checks from ordinary citizens, living in and loving an extraordinary place and wanting to make it better.

Tucson is home to a number of familiar names. Linda McCartney, of the rock and roll band Wings, and former spouse of Beatle Paul, lived in Tucson. Linda Ronstadt is one of a handful of celebrities calling Tucson home, but residents who know her brother, former Tucson Police Chief Peter Ronstadt, claim he has the best voice in the family.

Tucson has a thriving arts community. The resident professional Arizona Theater Company was conceived of around a kitchen table by Sandy Rosenthal, its Artistic Director, Marvin Cohen, Dino DeConcini, Carol DuVal Whiteman and the late Martin Ginsberg. Initially operating as the Arizona Civic Theater, it eventually began to perform its season in Phoenix as well as in Tucson. Tucson's Opera followed a similar pattern of development and it's symphony was the first such orchestra in Arizona by a number of years. And, of course, there is Old Tucson, the filming site of some of Hollywood's most famous movies. From western movie heroes like John Wayne to current box-office stars such as Harrison Ford, many of Hollywood's legends have walked these rugged streets. A number of prominent Hollywood figures now make Tucson their home.

Tucson has always had prominent families: Levy, Jacome, Grunwald, Brophy, Castro, and others. It might be a fortunate accident of being neither too big nor too small that it isn't just the prominent who are known for philanthropy. The "oblige" outweighs the "noblesse."

There was some indignant feedback when the Arizona Daily Star did a front-page story after Tucson resident Joe Bonanno died. Some citizens felt that Mafia figures shouldn't get that kind of attention. Most Tucsonans, however, have always been fondly tolerant of the reputation as the Mafia's western getaway. Put a few old Tucsonans together and they're likely to swap stories of seeing machine guns unloaded from a car behind a certain restaurant, or being at a well-known piano bar when several men entered firing machine guns. The Old Pueblo began with pistols in the saloons, and accepts that reputation as long as no one gets hurt.

Another family whose reputation and contributions are forever tied to Tucson is the Greenway clan. Among many accomplishments, the Greenways built the famous five-star landmark, the Arizona Inn. Patty Doar, granddaughter of the founder, first came to the Inn in the 1940's. She tells stories about her pioneering grandmother, Isabella Greenway King.

Isabella, best friend of Theodore Roosevelt's niece Eleanor, was a young widow with two children when she came to Arizona in 1922 on her honeymoon with former Rough Rider, John Greenway. Greenway had developed a new method for refining copper that made copper mining more profitable. Four years later Isabella was a widow once again when her husband died after surgery.

Isabella Greenway began making her name in Tucson through business and civic activities. She was elected Arizona's Democratic National Committeewoman and the state campaign chairman for Franklin Delano Roosevelt. In 1933 she won a special Congressional election, becoming Arizona's first and only Congresswoman. In the 40's she opened a furniture factory to give handicapped veterans a place to contribute and find dignity. Then she created a market to sell the furniture, and that market eventually became the elegant Arizona Inn Resort. For many Tucsonans, the Arizona Inn has become the heart of their community.

Many families carry on the tradition of holiday breakfasts at the Arizona Inn, including a pilgrimage to the huge tree in the library. Afternoon teas, weddings, and brunches weave like blossoms on a sampler through decades and generations. As steward of this site, Doar credits her Uncle Jack, Isabella's son, with instilling in her a sense of community.

"Once in a while, on a Sunday morning, we'd drive around town," she says. "He would explain the historic buildings, introduce me to people he knew. Uncle Jack loved the Hispanic history and Mexican culture. He had a nostalgic geography of downtown that he passed on to me."

But the best were his breakfasts.

"Everyone knew that Thursday morning breakfast was at Jack's. You never had to tell him if you were coming, you just had to appear before 8:30. All sorts of friends, people passing through town – you never knew who you would find there. Everyone came, and they all had stories to tell."

In Tucson's best tradition of "quiet giving," Doar remarks she didn't find out until after her uncle's death how many people he had assisted in the course of his life. "It wasn't just Uncle Jack," she says. "That sort of goodwill, and that connectedness – I find it everywhere in Tucson. If people are needed here, they get right to it. There's the feeling that there are things that can be done, and people don't wait to be asked to do them."

This aspect of Tucson pleases Doar, partly because it is in contrast to her years back East. She describes seeing a barefoot woman in a New York City winter and trying to find a way to help others like her.

"I went to a shelter for women, and asked what I could volunteer to do. They said everything was being handled by city agencies, not by individuals. But when I came to Tucson, I saw the opposite approach. I heard Nancy

Bissell and Gordon Packer explaining their vision of a men's shelter for the homeless. Then I watched them build it, stick by stick, into Primavera, where I finally had the satisfaction of joining a volunteer group."

Doar has a perspective on Tucson developed over decades. A lady in the classic sense, with modulated voice and inclusive spirit, Doar lights up describing the pleasure of seeing her grandchildren living here, learning the back hallways and gardens of the Inn she loves and calls home. Doar is no stranger to the world, having the infamous jurist Learned Hand as grandfather, and having married Watergate prosecutor John Doar.

Doar also mentions women like Dorothy Finley, Katie Dusenberry and Esther Tang as examples of civic contributors.

"Maybe it's because there is respect for women here. People have seen women run ranches, take over businesses when their husbands died. They are accorded a real respect. All these women who just stepped in and did what needed doing founded a wonderful part of Tucson. They were not, and are not, self-congratulatory."

Whether it is seeing luminarias glowing on gravel paths over the holidays or watching a monsoon build over the mountains in the summertime, Tucson is an amalgam of place and culture that goes deep in the hearts of its residents. Maybe the loyalty and affection is not unusual for a town, but it is remarkable for a town of this size. When only 50,000 people lived here, the feeling made sense. Now approaching a million, it makes less sense but is more precious.

Tucson may be growing up, and out, but not outgrowing itself. One can believe the residents who say, whatever new may be added, it will still be the same Old Pueblo to them.

ARIZONA INN

RON CAVIGLIA

ROUTE 66 RAILROAD

LA POSADA

CHAPTER 6

ROUTE 66 TOWNS:
TAKING A NEW DIRECTION

Route 66 meant freedom and opportunity to several generations of Americans. Commissioned in 1926, it became etched on the national consciousness just before World War II when in 1939 John Steinbeck referred to 'The Mother Road' in "The Grapes of Wrath." Then the catchy "Get your kicks on Route 66" provided a theme song for the daydream of setting out across the nation. Taking to the road, heading toward the sunset over the ocean, crossing the country seeking a better life, driving Route 66 seemed like a solution to anything not going right at home. From thematic gas stations to distinctive motels, Route 66 was more than a road; it was an ethos and an ideal. Then, thirty years after Steinbeck, a new anthem brought Route 66 into the awareness of a new generation: Dennis Hopper and Peter Fonda raced down Route 66 to the throbbing "Born To Be Wild" in Easy Rider.

But only fifteen years later Route 66 had been completely replaced by the four-lane Interstate 40. For slightly less than half a century, Route 66 was a concrete reality. In the 20 years since the last segment was closed near Williams, Arizona in 1984, the road has become part myth, part treasure, and part collective memory. For tourists, and the towns that served them, Route 66 is now seen through a rear-view mirror darkly. What was a lifeline for those communities is now a cultural memory. It can be recalled, but so far no one has figured out a way to bring it back.

For the towns that grew up on Route 66 and existed for tourists, every day since the Mother Road retired has been a struggle for her dependent children. For example, other than being immortalized in the Route 66 song between Oklahoma and Kingman, Wynona is just an exit sign near Flagstaff. Many of the old diners, motels and signs around Wynona lose a little more color and wood every year. From east to west, towns like Holbrook, Winslow, Williams, Ash Fork and Kingman have been abandoned by their earlier (some were mining or railroad towns first) purpose: to serve the westward pilgrims. Finding new directions to go has not been an easy path.

HOLBROOK

When you come into Arizona on Route 66 heading west, there isn't much except Holbrook. The Wigwam Hotel, one of the most familiar of all Route 66 landmarks with its white stucco teepees inviting residents to "go native" for a night, still stands. But Holbrook has been hit with a lot of bad luck in the last few decades. Interstate 40 diverted traffic from going through town, which hit tourism hard. A flood plain through downtown dried up grants and federal money for development. The population fell to about 5,000 people; of the three earlier grocery stores only one remains. But what works for Holbrook is the one thing that can literally bring a town back from the edge of oblivion, and that is a committed community.

Every town has what some call the "12 per centers." In any community about twelve percent of any population does 90 percent of the work. These energetic volunteers are the lifeblood of our entire nation. And there isn't a town in the United States that wouldn't be proud to have Glen Holden, one of the twelve percent, live there.

Holden chose Holbrook. Originally from Louisiana, he came west with his parents as a child and grew up in various White Mountain communities. He went to high school in Holbrook, playing football against the rival neighbor town of Winslow. After years working construction and traveling, he moved back because his mother still lived here. And when she died, he stayed. He had too much to do to move.

With a voice that rivals James Earl Jones, Holden could make the fine print in a law journal sound entertaining. Since he is by nature genial and looking for something to laugh at, everything he says seems delightful. But underneath that is a hard working, dedicated and determined man. He doesn't talk about it, but others tell of his one-man volunteer effort to collect junk mail for recycling. And how he does errands for those who can't get out. Even though he himself has been on disability since discs had to be removed from his back, Holden is dedicated to serving his town. He is the leader of Holbrook's Head Start program for the third year in a row, passionate about educating youth. He loves sharing the bounty from his garden – "It's amazing how you can grow just about anything here," he marvels. "Even peanuts. Eat some, save the seeds for next year."

Claudia Maestas, a close friend of Holden's, says it doesn't stop there. "Glen goes to Safeway and picks up produce, all kinds of stuff, for seniors," she says. "And he knows all these poor families, people who are handicapped, families with a lot of kids and not a lot of money. Cases of cabbage, ground beef, stuff on sale, he'll take them all to those folks. He's like a one-man grocery store that delivers, but never collects."

Holden is quick to say he's not alone. "I got a rancher friend who calls if a cow breaks a leg," he says. "He processes it at no charge, and I can take it around to people."

This kind of community support is inspiring and even hard to imagine to residents of large cities, where many people can't name four families on their street.

Holden created the organization "Holbrook Clean and Beautiful" a few years ago. "We started little cleanups around the city," he says. "We'd choose the 'clean and beautiful' yard of the month. A few people always show up."

Holden spearheaded a cleanup for Coastal Connection International, an organization to save waterways. With six volunteers, Holden took on the Little Colorado River near Holbrook, and got more than 3,000 pounds of debris out of the riverbed. "Everything from trees to car batteries to refrigerators," he chuckles. "You used to be able to catch a few catfish in the Little Colorado; now I know why you can't any more."

He says sometimes the heat of the high desert takes a toll. "It makes you wonder how early settlers made it here," he says. "Those people had to be tough. Those that made it." And they still do.

Holden was disheartened at the resistance he encountered revitalizing the town when he was Holbrook's vice-mayor. "I got a grant for ten thousand dollars," he recalls, "and people were afraid of change. They said, 'It's been this way for 40 years; if it ain't broke, don't fix it.' I said, 'Then let's break it and make it better.' We're at the mercy of corporate giants; we have one grocery store and the prices are killing us. People shop in Winslow where there are four grocery stores. Gas is ten cents a gallon cheaper in Snowflake. And you can't even get a pair of shoes in town."

Claudia Maestas was mayor when Holden was vice-mayor, and she nods her head as he talks. She agrees that it's tough, but there are people who are staying the course. She singles out hardware store owner Walt Portinir for not giving up. "He keeps a huge inventory here," she says. "And charges just a few percent more than the big chain hardware stores. Everyone tries to support him because he's such a good sport, and a very generous person."

Maestas says, when she was a child, Holbrook was a different place. There was so much traffic, that crossing Route 66 was dangerous. "Every kid in town, all summer long, would run back and forth to the store," she says. "You were dodging cars all the time. Now, you could run back and forth 40 times and never see a car. Losing Route 66 to I-40 was devastating. About 30 businesses shut down all of a sudden."

But she believes the worst is over. "Now that we have the levee built for the flood plain, there's money to go into downtown," she says. "I knew everyone in the Army Corps of Engineers working here by first and last name, by the time that got done. Now things are starting to go up. And the new paper plant at Joe City will provide 250 jobs for this area. Farmer John's has two pig farms coming in that will employ a lot of people."

Average annual salaries in Holbrook are about $30,000 – but the average home price is only double that. She wishes the city had been more aggressive in drawing industry, but doesn't think it's too late.

In the meantime, the community works to help itself. John Moore and his wife have tirelessly supported the Bread of Life Mission. He lights up describing how what began as five determined women "running around putting coats on everybody" sleeping outside in the winter, evolved into volunteers working out of an old Mobil station with mattresses. From there, it has evolved into a restored former church building that is used as a shelter with fulltime services for the homeless and hungry.

Unfortunately, the Moores recently had to put their house up for sale. Retired, they don't feel secure with the lack of medical facilities in Holbrook. Hospitals are too far away, and doctors are few. Moore regrets it, but he's moving to Chandler. "We're not alone," he says. "I can think of eight or ten good couples who have had to leave because of medical services. The town is dwindling."

In some ways it is. But the Elks, Rotary, Kiwanis, Lions and Masons are strong here. The PTA is very active. People leave doors unlocked and keys in their cars. And they not only love their neighbors, they love the place.

"Everyone supports one another," says Maestas. "Before you drive to another town to get something, you ask around to see what you can pick up for other people. Sometimes it's hard to find what they ask for, but you don't mind, because they do it for you. When a man in Joseph City had cancer, all the communities did fundraisers. Something tragic happens and people will band together up here. We understand shared experiences."

John Hatch has coached Little League for six years. He earned his degree in law at ASU thinking he would go into international business.

"But when I heard of a job opening with Navajo County," he says, "I knew that was mine. It's home here; I haven't wanted to leave. Even though," he adds, "If you meet someone who knows where Holbrook is, that's a very rare occasion." While he waits for the town to find a new direction to take toward growth and prosperity, he isn't missing the current pleasures it presents. "It's the sunrise and sunset," says Holden. "I've seen the sunset over the ocean, and even that's nothing like it is in the desert here. And the stars! On a clear night, you can see every star in the sky."

Esther Stang, longtime teacher in Holbrook, says it's the people that make this home for her. "My husband died five years ago," she says. "Every summer, some of the boys he coached in wrestling come over and mow my lawn. I always loved Northern Arizona." And she may have the best illustration of how Holbrook works its way into the hearts of residents.

"My husband was from Hawaii," she continues. "And we lived there for a while. He said he would move back and live all the days of his life here with me where I grew up, as long as I learned to cook Hawaiian food. I did; and we came home. We gave big luaus. But we would go to Hawaii to visit, and after we came home my husband would look around at Holbrook, and say, 'Now, this is paradise.'"

But not enough people feel this way to swell the population and industry.

Holbrook keeps tabs on how its neighbor to the west, Winslow, fares. With the recently refurbished La Posada Hotel and four grocery stores, there's some envy. Winslow also has almost doubled Holbrook's population and has drawn some of Holbrook's support services. "The gas company and cable company moved over there," says Maestas. "People here drive to Winslow to work at the prison, and to Snowflake to work at the paper mill. There's just been a decline here."

WINSLOW

Winslow's fortunes ebb and flow. On the plus side are the government and service headquarters, and the reopened La Posada, the crown jewel in the old Fred Harvey line of railroad hotels. While this lodge was designer Mary Colter's favorite of all Harvey lodges, it opened just after the Depression and never turned a profit. Longtime residents remember the sale of the signature "Mimbreño" china and rustic furniture. For years the La Posada served as Santa Fe Railroad headquarters. Now it's a resort again, drawing Route 66 history enthusiasts and other motorists, who stroll downtown and purchase Mother Road memorabilia.

Talk to residents and you find mostly people who are here by accident of birth and many young ones who are eager to leave for the "big city." At the annual Winslow Christmas parade, a young couple says they are both natives. The teenage boy cannot wait to move to a larger town with more going on. The young woman wants to move on too, but she plans to return to raise a family.

Loyal Winslow residents praise the close-knit feeling of a small town and diversity. Compared to the Arizona average, Winslow is more ethnically diverse. About a quarter of the population is Native American and five percent is African American. Hispanics and Anglos are more equal percentages than other places. Veterans, retirees and workers round out the demographics.

In Winslow some of the streets are dilapidated, with trash stuck against fences on empty lots; other streets are charming Midwestern rows of front porches and gabled roofs. Residence who celebrated birthdays at the town's Falcon Restaurant when they were children, can celebrate turning 50 at the same place, with the same view of the Mediterranean mural of a village, sea and sailboats.

The fire that destroyed the building on the famous "Standing on the Corner" landmark from the Eagles song, "Take It Easy" was a setback, but wasn't a knockout blow to the local economy.

Winslow's greatest hope for economic growth lies to the west in Flagstaff, where soaring property values might make Winslow, whose average home price is $60,000 appealing to those willing to make a half-hour commute.

FLAGSTAFF

Flagstaff, with Northern Arizona University, the Museum of Northern Arizona, Lowell Observatory and almost constant upscale home construction, doesn't depend as much on a Route 66 identity as some. On the edge of town, the Museum Club is a Mother Road relic and magnet for young partygoers and older tourists alike, and the numerous souvenir shops stock the obligatory Route 66 memorabilia. As the historical hub of Northern Arizona, Flagstaff warrants a full chapter – and gets one.

PARKS

Parks, the next community on old 66, is quickly becoming yet another bastion for summer homes. Property values are soaring, as California and Phoenix residents realize their dreams of owning land in pine country. The one-room store, formerly the biggest business, now seems tiny compared to the sophisticated roadhouse just off the Interstate. The biggest problem facing Parks according to some residents is that the absentee homeowners soundly reject regular efforts to raise taxes for education improvements in the local schools.

WILLIAMS

Williams is heading in a new direction – north. Thanks to the Grand Canyon Railway transporting passengers to the South Rim of the Grand Canyon, Williams has experienced a resurgence. Max and Thelma Beigert, who conceived of restoring the old depot and bringing steam engines back to the tracks in the 1980's, are heroes in Williams. The popular "Polar Express" Christmas holiday train rides and comfortable lodging like the Gadsden Hotel, restaurant and gift shop attract new fans from around the globe to Williams every year. And newly announced plans for a major theme park have the region excited.

Continue east across the state to Ash Fork, which might not exist if it weren't for the Mother Road. A truck stop is the only major building visible from Interstate 40. Most of the residents live in the rural surroundings and drive in for their mail. An administrator at Northern Arizona University marveled that when school children from the Ash Fork area came for a tour, he discovered that none had ever seen an elevator. On the other hand, all were conversant with the Internet.

KINGMAN

At the western end of Route 66's run through Arizona lies Kingman, and it's no accident that a sign provides mileage to other cities, showing how far it is to Laughlin and Phoenix. Kingman places itself in the context of being "on the way" to other destinations. But Kingman boasts being the hometown of some pretty big names. Andy Devine was a leading citizen. You may never have thought of Kingman as a romantic place, but apparently Clark Gable and Carole Lombard did, because Kingman is where they chose to get married! Now there isn't even a sign announcing you're entering Kingman when you exit off of Interstate 40.

Residents are laying groundwork to bring the good times back to town. Downtown merchants are already moving in a new direction; they offer tourists Seattle-quality coffee, lodgings that are both quaint and comfortable, and memorable dinners.

Richard Lansing grew up here, retired from the Navy and chose to move back after traveling the world. "You can't beat it," he says. "Sure, there are some islands out there that might have been nice, but they're the same year 'round. San Diego's nice, but the traffic goes five miles an hour on the freeways there. Here we get a dozen new residents a week, and they're retirees." He worries, however, "The kids say there's nothing to do here."

Kingman has an active adult community with an Elks Club, a Kiwanis Club, Soroptomists and Lions Club meetings. What it lacks is the bounty of jobs, although residents are excited about new businesses like Home Depot and a new business park by the airport, and they trade rumors about what jobs will be available, and when.

Now, Lansing says, Kingman has "a small town syndrome. In a depressed wage area, civic government is the top of the pecking order." Police and fire departments, and other city offices employ several thousand residents. But because rural offices pay less than cities, good employees often are lured away. Lansing laughs that he spoiled his son by finding him a job at the power plant in nearby Peach Springs that pays better than most white-collar work in the area.

He sees Route 66 as the goose that could lay golden eggs. "We need to get the right-of-way off 66. I'm old enough to remember how things were, and miss 'em. If the city spent more on tourism, out on the highways, we could do more." As it stands, the nearby casino in Laughlin makes it an attractive alternative for tourists.

Millie Morgan first lived in Kingman in 1966, left and came back. "It wasn't as big as it is now," she says, earnestly. While she wants others to appreciate the town, she realizes its limitations. "Hotel Brunswick downtown has a nice atmosphere, but there's no parking," she points out, practically. "Laughlin has cheap rooms because of the gambling. But being on Route 66 matters. That's how we're known."

She agrees with Lansing that it is the generation that remembers the lyrics, "Kingman, Barstow, San Bernardino, don't forget Winona," that is moving in. "Half of us are retirees. You can get a nice house for $100,000, and we like the good climate."

Morgan wishes the old town traditions could be brought back. "We had so many dances when I was first here," she says. "There was one every month anyway. People brought cakes and coffee. Now there's not really a place to do that." But by staying, Morgan hopes to be part of the renaissance, whenever it comes. "We accomplish something by living here," she says.

KINGMAN HOUSE

WIGWAM HOTEL, HOLBROOK

69

PRESCOTT PORCH

CHAPTER 7

PRESCOTT: OUT OF TIME

Welcome to Yesteryear. Welcome to Prescott.

The courthouse, columned and solemn, centered in the picturesque old Town Square park; the Hassayampa Inn's antiques and history; Senators Highway's enchanting Victorians, Sharlot Hall Museum's early homes, all are part of the charm of Prescott. It is possible to feel untouched by time looking at any of them.

In spite of the reassuring presence of the old buildings, Prescott has changed dramatically since a century ago, when cowboys would attempt to visit each of the dozens of saloons on Whiskey Row, consuming one drink at every bar. Boisterous and belligerent, they've been replaced by a population that is thoughtful and thorough about community life. Is the new mall a welcome sign of progress, or of greed? Are the country clubs and gated communities welcome or ruinous? All of it seems open to hot public debate in Prescott.

People are moving in droves to the mile-high town in East Central Arizona, bringing everything long time residents took for granted into question. How many support services are needed? Where and how should modernization come in?

Bob Hayne is a fairly typical new resident, whose eyes are merry and wise at the same time. He knows he can be seen as part of the problem. "I came from Southern California, which was too big and dirty," he says. "I was always drawn to the West, and when I drove down Gurley street the first time, my wife and I looked at each other and said, 'This is it.'"

Longtime Prescottonians and newcomers agree: the economic climate has changed. They recognize that those who can move from a large city and spend six figures on a home without blinking have raised property values beyond the reach of many in the working class. Vacant lots that would not have sold a decade ago because of traffic noise or steep slope now command high sales prices. Most young families or singles who keep the town businesses humming must drive in from the environs of Prescott Valley, Mayer or Chino Valley.

But Becky Ruffner, a member of Prescott's dynastic and historical family, says one of the new problems of prosperity is poverty.

"The city has a huge hidden poor," she says. "There are pockets of intractable poverty. There are no slums, but plenty of apartments and no low income housing. There are more than a thousand live births at Yavapai Hospital a year, and half of those mothers are under 22, single, and living at poverty level."

"It's sad the workers have to commute," says Kasey Hayne, a retired telephone company employee. "I love Prescott, but it's like how some people love their children; they say they're perfect regardless. Others love their children just as much, but still see how they could grow to become better." She says that there is real resistance to the changes. "I liken it here to folks who want to go back to the 50's. They don't welcome newcomers and change."

One resident was on the receiving end of that feeling. "I made the mistake of parking my fairly nice car at a polling place," he says. "When I came out after voting there was a note under the windshield wiper: 'You are one of those rich liberal do-gooders.' James Kimes learned from writing a letter to the editor that new opinions aren't always well received here.

"Progress was resisted," he says. "I said in my letter that all have a right to speak, and got a letter saying I should leave town for thinking that way." Fear drives that response.

Growth is relentless. You can't keep a child from becoming an adult; you just wish you could control the kind of adult he becomes. Prescott is like a young girl coming of age, leaving the farm to see the sights of the city. To her new friends in the flat above, her innocence and freshness are charming. But they also want her to come out with them, and will introduce her to the faster pace of city living, teach her to want the "latest" things. She will change, and they will think her more contemporary and acceptable.

To her parents seeing the transformation of the girl who steps off the bus on a visit, the changes may be horrifying. The new sophistication will have erased the lovely simplicity of the girl they raised. They will see the alterations as ruining, not enhancing, her. This differing perspective on sophistication is the schism between old and new residents.

Lee Nidess, also from California, says he's been accused of trying to bring California with him.

"It's a feeling I get. Why did I come here in the first place?" he says. "This is quite a place, with exceptional heritage. That it creates a tension is quite evident. There's a strong old boy network. But they have to grow; it's progress. You have to adapt to the right kind of things. If you don't grow, you decay."

The drive into Prescott from Interstate 17 along Highway 69 changes every year. More stoplights, more developments in formerly empty meadows, more franchise businesses appear annually. With them, of course, come more cars. Motels and restaurants are the overture for downtown, which manages to be the major tourist draw, and at the same time, proves difficult for many small businesses to make a living.

Murphy's remains. The traditional gathering place of homeowners and tourists alike still has the dark gleaming floors and casually elegant furnishings.

You can feel like a land baron of yesteryear sitting in the gleaming mahogany booths, candlelight glowing on lace and linen. You can picture debutantes with marcelled waves of shining hair posing on the staircase. And yet, newest citrus vodka is stocked at the bar. The best of old and new meld here.

Hayne says his neighborhood, Cliff Rose, welcomes the new without losing the turn-of-the-century, "Music Man" small-town feeling he loves.

"We found more friends in the first week living here than we did in 12 years back home," he says. "And if you're building a house you meet everyone, because they all wander through it."

Some say the city infrastructure can't keep up with the growth. Nidess, a former City Councilman, cites the homeless as an example.

"Their attitude is, 'Get 'em off the streets. We don't wanna see 'em,' " he says. "There are only 27 beds for the homeless here. That doesn't do it any more."

Another problem is the rising cost of medical care. Kasey Hayne says it's difficult for seniors because Medicare pays lower, rural rates in Prescott than in big cities.

"Doctors take the bite," she says. "Some physicians couldn't make it here, and went to Phoenix. The private insurance premiums are higher here. People who remain have to be absolutely sure they want to make the tradeoffs to live here."

But she says the cultural life of Prescott is far beyond expectations for the size of the city.

"We are season ticket holders for the symphony, and plays," she says. "The fine arts here are amazing. Yavapai College, the library, and even my little community of Cliff Rose, has more activities than any little subdivision. This town is full of closeness and caring."

While Prescott likes to call itself the Christmas City, for the traditional Courthouse Lighting Ceremony and Parade that to many Arizonans signal the opening of the holiday season, it's also the January City, when Phoenicians can drive less than two hours and descend wide-eyed on a foot of clean new snow, and figure out how to roll enough to start a snowman. It's the spring city, when flowers and trees bloom all around the Sharlot Hall Museum and everything feels dewy and new and laced with potential. It is the Fourth of July City, with the oldest continuous rodeo in Arizona. It is the Halloween City, with Senators Highway welcoming thousands of trick or treaters to the elaborately decorated old porches. Prescott is autumn leaves and summer evening breezes, welcoming warm hearths and the first daffodil.

Certainly if Prescott had an official town symbol, it would be the town square. With the gazebo gracing the wide lawn, the statue of Bucky O'Neill, the high clock and sandstone construction, and the courthouse lawn is timeless and inviting. On postcards, decked with lights during the holidays, crowded with spectators for the Fourth of July parade, the courthouse square says "Prescott" to residents and visitors alike.

The courthouse square is Prescott's Statue of Liberty, extending an invitation to visitors and third-generation residents alike to rest on the grass, stroll the sidewalks, climb the stairs and slide down banisters polished by years of enthusiasm.

Sharlot Hall Museum is where buildings go to retire. The Fremont House and the Bashford House date back to the 1870's, and the Governor's Mansion and a rustic room called "Fort Misery" a decade before. People love to wander the Museum rooms, furnished with period pieces and steeped in history. One advantage to a city rich in retirees is always having enough docents – as well as other volunteers. People who can choose where they want to live after they stop working bring energy, expertise and an understanding of the value in helping others.

"The volunteers are the shining stars of this community," says Caroline Drost. "Volunteerism is above and beyond anything I've seen." She adds that city services are generally good across the board.

Becky Ruffner agrees. "My window overlooks the Plaza, which is the heart and soul of the community." Also the library. "Every color, age, demographic goes in and out those doors. I can't imagine a more diverse collection of people."

And not everyone moving in has retired. Veterans come for the hospital, and find a peer group living close by. Dot-com moguls who can work from anywhere that has a high-speed Internet connection and a good coffeehouse are charmed by the authenticity and atmosphere. Outdoor lovers get dizzy from the variety of hiking trails, natural scenery and accesses to wide-open spaces and stay. Young couples affluent enough to raise their children in an environment away from large cities see neighborhoods with each home different and start looking for the one with their lawn they want the children to run across.

But residents like Prescott for what's outside the city limits as well.

Doris Cellarius, who looks both vibrantly healthy and elegantly natural, moved here four years ago.

"I walk in the woods," she says. "I like where I live. The fact that I can live in a town where I can walk to the forest, or the post office, is good." She is involved with Creekside, a local group making sure the waterways stay clean and accessible, another example of the cadre of volunteers who are able to do so much beyond what local government can fund.

"The rolling hills are gorgeous," says Vicky O'Hara, who moved to Prescott after her children grew up and left home. "You get four seasons here, none harsh, and cool summer nights. It's just a beautiful place. We have lakes and great trails."

Prescott doesn't have a choice about whether or not to grow: outsiders are assuring that it will. It does have a choice however, about how involved to become in the process. Time and again, the people who feel most powerless and complain the most are those who have not become deeply involved in the workings of the town. Those who show up for public meetings, sit on boards, volunteer for cleanups, radiate a peace and acceptance from being part of the process. They may not like all the changes in store, but they will do all they can to ensure they approve of a majority.

The trick, and all the residents want to perform it but cannot agree on how, is to keep the history and flavor of pioneer Prescott, while adding the conveniences and services needed by progressive Prescott.

Two facets of Prescott come out of time: One is the Governor's Mansion, which has been through almost a century and a half of storms and change, and still endures; the other the scattering of ghosts who supposedly startle and charm guests at several local hotels and bed-and-breakfasts. They, too, have managed to survive the growth, at least by reputation. Prescott sets a good example for its people when it comes to living through change, and show that important things can be preserved, before residents run out of time.

PRESCOTT MUSEUM LAWN

UNITED STATES & NAVAJO FLAGS

CHAPTER 8

THE NAVAJO:
LONG WALK IN BEAUTY

Navajoland is spare, wide, dramatic country covering the northeast corner of Arizona. It is a country of little water and unbridled openness. The living desert scenery is subtle to first-time visitors: some scrub, a brush of green indicating a spring or seep. Occasionally a dwelling: either a traditional six-sided hogan, or often a mobile home or small cinderblock house. Vast stretches of seemingly endless road see few cars and most of those are pickup trucks. But those who love this area savor the limitless sky, with its masterpiece clouds; the shading of sandstone through brown, peach and salmon striations. This is land with room to breathe, time to move slowly, space in nature, this country promises. And it is under the sovereign Navajo Nation.

To understand the Navajo Way could take decades of study. But to understand the subtle reserve with regard to Anglo visitors on the reservation can be accomplished in a few minutes.

Go back to 1863, two years after a peace treaty was signed between Navajo leaders and the United States government. Kit Carson, the famous western scout, embarked on a slash-and-burn campaign against the Navajo people. Reading about it evokes images of recent incidents of African ethnic cleansing: soldiers riding into villages setting homes on fire; destroying crops and livestock so if there were survivors, they would starve. Women and their small children trying to escape were murdered. Some believe this slaughter was due in part to Eastern capitalists taking interest in mineral wealth on Navajo land, which would be easier to appropriate if cleared of the Navajos. Certainly James H. Carleton, one of the government officials steering the Indian policy at the time urged soldiers to prospect along their way and report back on any silver or ore veins discovered.

Navajos living farthest west had the best luck in escaping the U.S. Cavalry. Hiding in small slot canyons and on mesas in Arizona, thousands managed to elude the soldiers. Troops could ride through snowy country and rough terrain, but they didn't know the secret places of the wide, spare wilderness the way the tribe did.

About 8,000 Navajos were eventually rounded up and ordered travel about 300 miles to the east to be resettled. This trek was called "The Long Walk," and mentioning it to a Navajo can be compared to saying "Auschwitz" to someone of the Jewish faith. Hundreds died on the trail. Not told by their captors how to prepare flour or coffee, they mixed the former with water to drink, and tried to roast the coffee beans to eat. Weakened, hungry and sick, those who fell behind were often either shot in the snow or left to die.

Those who survived the trip faced conditions in the camp that were almost as desperate. Men were forced into slave labor. Some escaped, more died in blazing summers and freezing winters with little in the way of shelter or nourishment.

Four years after it began, the U.S. Army wrote off the whole venture as a bad job. Reduced by perhaps a quarter of their number (records were sketchy and not well preserved), the Navajo left their prison camp and began the journey home. According to oral histories, many of them kept expecting to be captured and brought back. Survivors said it wasn't until they saw the San Francisco Peaks, long held as sacred to the Navajos, before they finally believed they were being allowed to return to their homeland.

Thinking about this grim history, one approaches the reservation with some reluctance, some hesitation, and some shame. What one finds are gracious people, whose cultural and social dynamics are strikingly different from our own. For example, you don't meet someone's eyes when you speak; to do so could be disrespectful. Navajo are private people, and are hesitant to express personal opinions and stories like so many of us seem eager to do.

Just south of Interstate 40 approaching the Navajo Reservation, you pass a sign indicating that the small group of buildings on your right is called Witch Well. It's a tavern, mostly. A few miles north is Sanders, a slightly larger gathering of buildings as unpretentious and utilitarian as Witch Well.

Walk up to the Burnham Trading Post in Sanders on the southern edge of the Navajo reservation, and the first door you encounter has a sign: "Please use other door." (Likewise next door at the Route 66 Diner.) You can come in, but you have to make the effort.

Under such circumstances, a guide is a godsend; someone to interpret, explain, and make sure you don't commit an unwitting social gaffe. Bruce Burnham is a fourth-generation Anglo Indian trader and husband to a Navajo woman for 45 years. The sharp-eyed but genial Burnham has loved and embraced the Navajo culture since his boyhood, and he is willing to share some of his observations and perceptions.

You might talk in the back room of Burnham's trading post. Not the Anglo version of a trading post, but a place with utilitarian tin coffee pots, dishes and skillets in blues and whites, flour sacks, and auto supplies. Three walls are arrayed with abundant shades of wool to be woven on looms. There is a case of "dead pawn" jewelry: A Navajo who needs money can leave a piece of jewelry as collateral, and when the time for the money to be paid back has passed, the jewelry can be sold. Burnham will buy dead pawn from other traders, but never sell the pieces he has taken from Navajos.

"We save all the old pieces for the families," he says. "That's something that means so much to them. It behooves us to get along in a community this small. We want to get along with everybody."

Both clerks and shoppers fall silent and just watch when someone from out of town walks through the door. But Burnham's clerk offers an introduction to her boss as someone who doesn't mind talking. This man is a bridge to a largely unknown society, an interpreter of social customs as deeply and delicately rooted in respect and tradition as anything European nations ever produced.

Burnham grew up at Grey Mountain and then Dinnebito. He began his informal introduction to Navajo ways by playing cards with the older Navajo men who would come down to the trading post and sit around a table in the bull pen, the large central circle of space in a trading post.

The card game, says Burnham, was called "koon cain," and he wasn't very good at it.

"I never really learned to play, and every time I played I lost money," he says. "But I figured I was payin' for my entertainment. All the Navajos' bantering taught me the language. They took me under their wing. I was there to learn. I didn't try to make them instruct me. I spent forty years observing."

Those years of observation gave Burnham a priceless credibility and comfort level with his customers. A woman comes into the trading post dressed in the classical garb of Navajo women of a certain age: velvet skirt, printed cotton blouse, running shoes, head scarf and wire-rimmed glasses. Burnham addresses her in fluid Navajo, and she smiles with her whole face and answers him. You can tell he is regarded as doon eh' – clan. Because the culture is matriarchal, his children are identified as Navajo. He is considered as clan because of his integration into the nation.

After living on the reservation for a number of years, Burnham once got restless, and left the reservation for a time.

"You have to go and come back," he says. "I ran the trading post in Aneth, on the southern edge of Utah. Every day I'd get up and open at eight a.m. I saw the same old Indian ride the same old horse right into the store. He was the only punctual Indian I ever met; you could set your clock by him.

"He'd get a little can of tobacco and a grape Nehi. The soda would make his mouth sting, and he'd spit on the floor. I'd clean up. That was his routine. That was my routine. I really admired the old goat; so constant, so straight.

"But I was 24 years old, and one day I thought, 'Here I am, stuck in the bowels of the world, which is going a thousand miles an hour, and I'm stuck. I threw the keys on the counter and quit."

Like many his age, Burnham found Haight-Ashbury in the height of hippie culture. He also found the Indian Club in Oakland.

"We'd go butcher a sheep for mutton, and make fry bread; anyone who went home had to haul a bag of Bluebird flour back," he said. "And after a year and a half I went back to work for the same guy in Aneth, and never ever had a desire to leave. I'd never seen the beauty of this country till I came home."

After the marriage to an Anglo failed, ("She couldn't stand the reservation and I couldn't stand living in town") Burnham was single for eight years. But not without a dream.

"My brother asked me when I'd ever get married again, and I said if I did, I want to marry someone like Virginia Deal. But she was fifteen at the time. Well, four years later, I was able to call him and tell him, 'I'm getting married tomorrow."

One of the most engaging things about Burnham is that when he describes his marriage ceremony 40 years ago, he becomes hushed and reverent.

"A traditional Navajo wedding ceremony is the most meaningful thing that can happen to a man," he says. "It was very spiritual."

The marriage is arranged between the wife's family and the husband's uncle. Burnham's boss stood in and worked out the dowry.

"In my case, that was a cow, a Concho belt and a new car I paid for her."

Then Burnham's friends and relatives were supposed to come to the bride's home for several days.

"All my Navajo friends, a lot of the older medicine men and the bootlegger were hanging out and playing cards before the wedding. Half got drunk and passed out, and didn't make it."

But the half that did shared in what Burnham calls "a very functional ceremony."

"Everything serves a purpose. The entourage comes to the woman's house because all the man's obligations go to the family. Her family gains a worker. The medicine man sat us men down and explained what my responsibilities would be. The whole ceremony was focused on me, cluing me in to what to expect."

Then the man and woman come together. Burnham blessed a basket of corn pollen, and drew a line in the pollen from south to north, and from east to west. He put a line all around the basket with a small opening, to symbolize free agency. The couple both ate out of each direction, and the groom washed his hands four times over the ground, symbolizing the food and people coming from and returning to the earth. The bride did the same, and then the basket was passed through the crowd.

"Everyone had to eat. Everyone had to participate; it was a way of blessing the union. Kind of like saying, 'Speak now, or forever hold your peace.' "

Burnham wasn't regarded as an outsider, but his new in-laws were aware his clan had different tastes.

"They had a huge feast, and tried to have everything white people would want: yeast rolls, Waldorf salad, roast turkey, ham, beef," he says. "Then for the Navajo side was mutton stew, sheep intestines cleaned and filled to make blood sausage, and fry bread. So all the Navajos showed up and went for the Waldorf salad, and all the whites were over on the other side eating mutton stew and fry bread."

Burnham is crusty but affable. He doesn't mince words when expressing his disdain for Navajo wannabes and do-gooders. To earn the trust of the people is not something done in an afternoon. Spend 20 years, and Burnham will credit you with willingness.

He disparages current attempts to replace the Mexican word "Navajo" with the tribal "Dineh," meaning "The People." "Dineh has a really powerful meaning," he says, "But we're still Navajos. We have ceremonies in Navajo. Saying dineh instead is about going out and getting people unhappy about how we're treated." While not all Navajos share his view, Burnham says everyone he knows uses "Navajo."

Another current term he disparages is "The Rez." He believes that, "On the reservation, it sounds too light-hearted. It's a little bit derogatory."

A widely held opinion among Navajos is that the biggest disservice Anglos ever did the Navajo tribe – even though it may have been well-intentioned – was taking children off the reservation and sending them to schools.

Burnham says: "Loss of language means loss of oral tradition. I know things have to change – there's too many Navajo to survive on a herd of sheep – but they took away tradition. There is no culture more respectful or polite than Navajo, but teachers took it away and taught Emily Post."

He uses the example of teaching young Navajo students to say "please."

"We have a word: a sho'nd. It's the most powerful word in the Navajo culture. If someone utters that word, the other person doesn't have the agency of freedom to say 'no.' But by making it like using 'please' it took away the power. Navajos know we are responsible for helping each other. But if you use a sho'nd and aren't entitled to receive, maybe your luck would be bad. Maybe the slice of bread you ask for won't be nourishing. You would pay somehow down the line. And yet kids were taught to say please, to beg. Can you imagine what that did to the culture? The religious connotation was destroyed."

He adds that the Anglo habit of labeling beliefs as superstitions is common and unfair. "The reluctance to go where chindii, the spirit, still exists after a death, that's not a superstition. It's the very essence of being Navajo."

He maintains that Navajo are not shy people, but come from a culture with elaborate manners and traditions. The reason most Navajos are reluctant to explain their beliefs is that ideas are regarded as sacred. "If you speak it, it gives life to it. For as long as someone is alive who remembers it said, it's still alive. We're giving birth to what we say, and are accountable for that. You can attribute it to shyness, but it's really accountability. You may want the deep side of Navajo, but Navajos won't say it." As everywhere, the young people's lack of adherence to their parents' ways keeps every culture gradually shifting from the way it was a century ago. And considering how drastically culture off the reservation has changed in 100 years, the Navajo are working to keep their young people involved in the culture.

A surprising element of the outside world is leading young Navajos back to their roots: Hip-hop.

Patrick Burnham, Bruce's 22-year-old son, seeks out the old legends now in a way he never has, and uses them in songs and raps he writes. He says his peers respond to hip-hop like basketball, another aspect of urban street culture Navajos embrace. One reason is that Navajos are often solitary, living in homes or small communities with few friends. Both hip-hop and basketball can be solitary as well as group activities. But hip-hop offers more.

"Hip-hop gives kids a link to something larger than themselves," says Patrick. 'They can be part of the reservation and part of something else." He thinks the themes of feeling cut off from the mainstream, looked down upon and being eternally an outsider resonate to the young Navajos.

"It helps release desperation, bitterness, the futility of not being able to attain higher levels," he says. Hip-hop gives voice to the feeling of being caught between two worlds. It also mirrors chanting while moving in a circle, the pattern of Navajo ceremonies. Dance battles in hip-hop echo traditional healing ceremonies and celebrations.

"Rappers or MC's are like our storytellers."

Recently Patrick wrote a piece called "Fifth World Order," harkening back to the Navajo legend of the tribe's passage through four worlds before reaching this one.

"Hip-hop parallels the Navajo tradition, and makes us want to return to our roots and learn from the elders," he says. While the themes are tribal, the chosen language is still English.

"I heard one guy do it in Navajo, and it sounded really weird," Patrick says. A website shows schedules for hip-hop and dance competitions, and photos of young Navajos performing. Names like Sheephead, Wicked X Coalition, Horny Toads and Body Part Rain result from blending two disparate heritages.

Burnham watches his son leave for a dance competition and shakes his head fondly. The young man wears two earrings and a t-shirt with a slogan whose meaning is obscure to many. But when asked, Burnham says he believes his son will follow in his footsteps and take over the running of the trading post— a fifth generation Indian trader and the first with co-mingled blood. It doesn't get much better than that for the man who loves the Navajos: his son carrying on his tradition and finally joining him to the people he loves.

It would be impossible to talk about the Navajo culture without also talking about the Hopi tribe. While their origins differ – Navajos of

Athabascan origins, and Hopis claim Pima heritage – the tribes are inter-twined, for good or ill.

The much smaller Hopi reservation is completely surrounded by Navajo land. The most troubling matter between the tribes involves about three-quarters of a million acres of land that both tribes claim they own. (This sounds like a huge area, but is actually a small portion of Navajo land.) This dispute, beginning in the 1960s, is one of the longest federal lawsuits in American history. It has involved evicting Navajos from their homes, preventing Hopis from visiting sacred sites, and creating acrimony between those living in the disputed area. While most of the issues have been solved, the acrimony lingers.

Navajos and Hopis have other stress points, such as the vaunted Navajo Code Talkers that helped win World War II in the Pacific by using their language as a code that never was broken by the Japanese. There were Hopi Code Talkers as well; the tribe maintains that the natural modesty of their culture has kept this group from getting deserved credit.

Hopis live on Second Mesa, where Old Oraibi is believed to be the oldest continuously inhabited village in the United States. Navajos are more scattered across the largest reservation created, in both Arizona and New Mexico.

Some Hopi and Navajo intermarry, like Hopi Emerson Horace, who has a Navajo wife. Raised on the reservation, Horace attended school there until moving to the parochial school at Ganado in third grade, where his father worked for famous Indian trader Lorenzo Hubbell at his trading post.

The pattern of choosing education over home continued; first at Northern Arizona University, then to Penn State for a masters in education administration. Horace smiles when he says he's one dissertation chapter short of a doctorate degree.

The conflict between the traditional ways of the Hopi, and the struggle to survive in the modern world is felt by all of Arizona's tribes. It is a delicate balance to educate young people to move into the modern world without losing all ties to the old ways. For the Hopis, this includes everything from keeping traditional ceremonies while Jehovah's Witnesses and Assembly of God churches dot the area, to figuring out what to do about unsightly power lines where digging in the ground might violate sacred objects.

"Our people are our own worst enemies," he says. "I see a lot of change coming, and we could be leading it instead of having it just happen to us."

While advocating progress and eschewing life on Second Mesa, Horace carries a strong love for his homeland and a desire to help the tribe survive. He is working to promote a project that he believes would bring the benefits of both new and traditional culture to his people.

When Horace goes home to Second Mesa, he sees the slapdash, scattershot construction of modern rooms added on to the elaborate stonework ancient dwellings,

"Hopis are really good masons, but the art has kind of died out," says Horace. "One thing I've wanted to do is bring back masonry; start a high school vocational program where the elders teach stone work. They could use the young workers to renovate the old villages, and make houses to replace mobile homes. Those are really an eyesore."

But so far, Horace hasn't been able to get enough of the right people excited and involved.

"Our people move so slowly," he says. "They take every single little thing into consideration before making a decision."

Some progressive Hopis are frustrated by the older village elders' reluctance to look at new ways of generating income. The Hopi are dependent on Peabody coal contracts, which Horace says supply about three-quarters of the tribe's income, and which has a very uncertain future. Should Peabody close, the job losses and economic dislocation will be drastic, and accelerates the need for diversification.

One way progressives have dealt with the issue is by investing in off-site properties that would surprise most outsiders. The Hopi tribe owns not only large cattle ranches in Northern Arizona and a factory outside Winslow, but also the Kokopelli Inn in Oak Creek, the large truck stop outside Holbrook, the Flagstaff community of Kachina Village and even Heritage Square in downtown Flagstaff.

The Hopi and the Navajo people are rich cultures with extraordinary traditions and history. They are facing an increasingly threatening future, and both are working with creativity to find a balance between protecting their heritages, and moving forward into the future.

TRADING POST

BRUCE BURNHAM

STEVE UDALL

UDALL HOMESITE

CHAPTER 9

ST. JOHNS:
ESTABLISHING ROOTS

T he Church of Jesus Christ of Latter-day Saints made its contribution to Arizona lore not with a pen, but wagon tracks. Sent by Brigham Young to scout the area and find town sites, early Mormons carved a living out of inhospitable country, making the desert blossom like the rose with irrigation, imagination and backbreaking work.

Sent out first from Salt Lake or St. George in Utah, early Saints traveled by horse, wagon or even foot, to empty territory where they could colonize and worship freely. The route traced across the Kaibab Plateau on the Arizona Strip, and through rocky, unforgiving ridges. It became known as the "Honeymoon Trail," because couples who wished to have their marriages sealed in the Utah Temple had to travel the convoluted route back, including the backbone of cliffs leading to the Colorado River crossing named Lee's Ferry, for another church member, John D. Lee.

Having been driven from wary and even violent eastern and midwestern communities, Mormons craved safe places more than almost anything. Towns like Heber, Winslow, Eager, and Thatcher were established far away from settled areas. Typically this meant the sites were even more hardscrabble than average. But the early Saints demonstrated a sure hand at channeling water to grow crops, and weren't afraid to create the necessary channels in unforgiving caliche. Bringing brick, buying or cutting timber, and carrying rock, the families created homes where they could raise their many children and worship with like-minded brethren.

Throughout their history, Mormons have proven to be resilient and sturdy – in their religion and in their character. Arizona is a different place for the many significant contributions of the LDS church, and for the disciplined and family-oriented philosophy Saints bring to their communities.

Some of those towns have been absorbed into other communities, like Joseph City into Winslow. Others, like Mesa, have kept some of their original culture. Many of these towns, especially on the eastern side of the state, retain much of their founders' stamp.

St. Johns (no apostrophe – he doesn't own it) is a prototypical Arizona Mormon settlement. With the distinctive wide streets (laid out so a horse team and wagon could turn around without going to a corner) and hosts of trees, St. Johns looks somewhere between bucolic, and stuck in the 1940s.

St. Johns is not large, and is noticeably free of franchises. Auto repair shops, hotels and markets boast the kind of unique names you see mostly on reruns of "The Waltons." Walk into one lobby, and the entire ceiling is festooned with the green loops of philodendron plants that have been patiently trained over the years to weave across the tiles. It's an interesting and slightly bizarre feature that wouldn't last long in a metro downtown. Gardens fill some lots between houses, and you don't have to drive far to be looking at wide empty land.

Located in the middle of Apache County, one of the most desolate and least populous areas in Arizona, St. Johns doesn't have the dazzle of a natural wonder to entice tourists to visit. There is a museum, touching in its earnestness. Walking through it, you figure whatever members or committee accepted donations wanted to capture the eclectic spirit of the town. Some of the displays may seem a bit homey. Yet in the neighboring cases, intricate displays illustrate the early native tribal life of the area, the area's Mexican history, and relics of typical frontier manhunts and hangings.

If you get out of your car and wander into the Busy B, a restaurant with wide windows and red plastic cups, you feel as if you've stumbled into Garrison Keillor's fictional Chatterbox Café. This is where residents come to exchange gossip, reminisce and have a drink or a meal. St. Johns, like other fortunate small towns, is all about the people.

Scratch the surface of any Mormon community, and you find ties to other towns and families. Mention John D. Lee, who not only established Lee's Ferry but also was a high-ranking church member, and it turns out three of the six people sitting at the table at the Busy B are related to him. Mention Pipe Spring National Monument, an old fort set up by the early LDS church, and three of them are related to the first telegraph operator in the state. Not only that, but their ties to other families in the area include names less well known, and a knowledge of bloodline and heritage that would impress even a Scottish clan chief.

St. Johns was called San Juan before the Mormons arrived in 1880: Mexican Catholics were the primary population. There was bad blood in the early years. The church headquarters in Salt Lake City actually gave the LDS pioneers permission to end their settlement because resentment ran high from the established Catholics. The town was completely separated by blood and belief.

"On the white Mormon side, the prejudice was racial," Steve Udall says. "On the Catholic Hispanic side, it was religious."

The Mormon church reasoned there was safety in numbers, and sent 100 more families to St. Johns. Sure enough, with the population more evenly balanced between Hispanic Catholics and Anglo Saints, tension subsided. The joke in St. Johns is, "The weak stayed in Utah, and the tough came here."

To talk about St. Johns is to talk about Udalls. No other small town in Arizona (and maybe no big one) has produced as many judges, legislators and public servants. Check any website of those who have worked in government, and there's a huge paragraph of Udalls, going back to David King Udall, one of the patriarchs of St. Johns and an Arizona pioneer.

Born in 1851, D.K. Udall rose quickly through the ranks of the fairly young Mormon Church, becoming a high priest in his mid-20s. The young man was sent to St. Johns as a newly ordained bishop, where he was not only in charge of the spiritual development of his flock of Mormon pioneers, but also constructing irrigation ditches, mills, and a school for the community.

D.K. Udall's road was not a smooth one: he was sentenced to a federal prison for perjury about a fellow Mormon's land claim, although he later received a full pardon from President Grover Cleveland. His two wives had a rocky relationship, and money wasn't always easy to come by. Even so, he made time for a term in the Arizona Territorial Legislature, and imprinted upon his eleven children and beyond, a strong commitment to public service.

Two of his sons, John Hunt and Levi Stewart, were on the Arizona Supreme Court, and another, Jesse Addison, was a mayor of Phoenix. Grandson J. Nicholas was a superior court judge. Another grandson, Stewart Lee, was Secretary of the Interior under President John Kennedy. A third grandson, Morris King, was the beloved Democratic congressman for three decades, who ran for president in 1976. Known as Mo to Arizonans, this was the Udall who gained a national following for his self-deprecating humor and countrified yet incisive bromides that made him a modern Mark Twain.

Three other great-grandsons, Thomas, Mark, and Gordon, also served in Congress. A grandson, Steve, was district attorney in Apache County. He joins a group for breakfast to talk about his hometown. It seems appropriate that half the people at the table are Udall relatives.

Spence and Cameron are Steve's son and daughter. Both tanned and vigorously attractive, they share their father's easy-going humor. Mo Udall may have been the most famous, but all of the Udall family appear to be expansive, genial, and at the same time sharply focused on civic duty and human behavior.

The Udall family home, where the illustrious generations were raised, is next to the Busy B. In front of it, a landmark oak spreads thick branches over the street. Cameron, or Cam, described the clan having a centennial birthday party when the tree turned 100, "with five generations singing 'Happy Birthday' in the front yard."

Some Udalls left and returned;. Steve earned his law degree at ASU but moved home to raise his family. His years with the County Attorney's office were busy, since Apache County is large and remote. Udall took the work seriously, but his career is punctuated with anecdotes that would do Mo proud.

One was that he was prosecuting a man from Holbrook for cattle rustling.

"I got him on the stand," says Steve, deep laugh lines already fanning out from his eyes, "and I said to the judge, 'You know, while Tex is on the stand, he's under oath. Well, his wife is here, and she'd like to ask him a few questions, too.' The judge didn't think it was a bit funny, but the courtroom roared."

The downside to his position was that "I never prosecuted a case where I didn't know someone involved," he says. "If you're going to be a cop or prosecutor around here, you better be polite and treat people right. You'll see them again." That's because while few new families move here, few old ones leave.

"For eons, the population of St. Johns stood right at 1300," says Steve. "The only time that changed between the 1880s and today was during the Depression." At that time population doubled with young men coming home to help out of the farm, where food and shelter were available. Current population stands at around 3,000, but most of them trace to the original families.

Those who aren't related to Udalls are connected other ways. Bethany Cherry, a young mother of two, is the granddaughter of St. Johns native Ivan Cherry. "When I was county attorney," Steve says, "Ivan was the only probation officer in court system, period."

The two reminisce about Ivan's famous pack trips, and Steve recalls that when asked how Ivan lost the tip of his little finger, he would tell small children that something horrible bit it off while he picked his nose, probably creating manners in several generations of townsfolk.

An exception is Keirsten Neilsen, who is married to Fred Neilsen, Spence Udall's business partner. A shy but striking woman with fair skin and midnight hair, Keirsten could be modeling in New York instead of raising kids in St. Johns. But she loves her life.

"I don't have any blood relatives here," she says. "But I'd always loved visiting St. Johns. I liked the green grass and trees. Everybody knows you, even before I knew them. You get invited to do things. I've been here two years now, and I absolutely love it. If I go away, when I come over that hill and see the town, I'm home."

Keirsten says living in St. Johns melds old and new ways.

"I'm a web shopper now," she says, since the town shops are small and anything bigger is at least an hour away. But while her purchases are ordered by means pioneers could not have comprehended, they would see at Keirsten's house a vegetable garden similar to theirs, and would spend summer days canning, as she does.

Kiersten met her husband Fred at NAU in Flagstaff. They've been purchasing property they hope to renovate, to bring new life to the town. Spence says many young people want to leave, and only some come back.

"There's no place to spend money here. As soon as your kids smell gasoline and perfume, they go to pot," he says affably. "I guess I was too dumb to want to leave. But parents of kids who do come back worry. There just aren't jobs, and they don't want to see us starve. We took a pay cut to come back here and start a business, but we want to invest our money here, and raise our families here."

Spence flourishes in the small town.

"It's like you're all family. You can leave your checkbook in the car. I'm an EMT, and I leave the keys in the car at night so if I get called out I don't have to look for them. If cars stop in the middle of the road to talk, you don't interrupt, you just go around."

He thinks there's some room for St. Johns to grow, however.

"The old-timers say 'We don't want to be another Phoenix,' but we could use about two hundred more families without having to worry about that," he says with a broad grin.

St. Johns prides itself on keeping the past alive. Pioneer Days is a summer celebration complete with an ice cream social in the park, and the town population triples that week. The tiny town museum contains photographs of early Mormon and Hispanic families, old garments and tools. Fred and Cam Udall feel the importance of family legacies. In a town where the saying goes, "The only thing dumber than a cow is the guy who owns one," Fred still keeps the old ranch property – but not for cattle.

"My great-grandpa homesteaded this land, and raised 13 children," he says. "There's just a section left, with the old house. The ranch is a place for the family to get together. Now it has memories instead of cows."

Saints, Hispanics and others live and work side by side in today's St. Johns. Time and proximity have loosened the strict separation of Catholic and Mormon residents. Weddings now have both celebrating the joining of their families. This may be in part because while the religious doctrine of the two cultures is vastly different, the strong dedication to family dominates both.

Cam says there was a time she took St. Johns for granted.

"When I brought a friend back from law school to visit, I showed him my great-grandparents house," she says. "And the family's books that are 200 years old. He said, 'You have no idea what you have here. I'd give anything for this kind of family and history.' Now I know there are two things in life: One, knowing who you're people are; and two, accepting it."

Not everyone is comfortable with some precepts of the Church of Jesus Christ of Latter-day Saints. But it would be difficult to leave the convivial, comfortable group and the Busy B without a regret that you aren't part of it; you don't have a family home here, and you won't be coming back for Pioneer Days this year. Those who will belong to something rare, rich and precious.

ST JOHNS TREE ARCH

BISBEE STREETSCAPE

CHAPTER **10**

MINING TOWNS:
AFTER THE ORE:

Through the 1960's Arizona schoolchildren were taught state commerce as "The Five Cs". These were cattle, citrus, climate, copper and cotton. Copper was truly king of them all.

Today, of the five, climate may be the most profitable, drawing tourists and new residents in droves. Cotton still grows and is harvested as world famous Pima cotton, said to be as luxurious as Egyptian cotton. Citrus and cattle have as many detractors as supporters in Arizona, depending on where water allocations go, and who profits from them. But copper has been Arizona's most visible contribution to the national economy, so much so that it was once boasted you couldn't find a penny that wasn't made with Arizona copper.

But an "extraction economy," taking out natural resources for money, is tenable at best. Whether water, oil, minerals or land, Arizona has finite stores of its riches. Through the 1800's, thousands of prospectors filed claims in what is now Arizona. Towns sprang up around the richest mines, and settlements at the smaller ones. Some of them still survive.

At one time, every one of Arizona's numerous ghost towns expected to flourish. Maps show them in each county, and you can read about the fine buildings and prosperous residents that have long disappeared. Few people remember where Algert, Gold Basin, Red Rover or Senator stood. The town of Pioneer in Gila County, like nearby Globe, at one time had a school, brewery, hotel, bank, stores and many residents. Clarkston, to the west, had 1,500 residents, a movie theater, newspaper, hotels and stores – not unlike the services offered in Globe today. Post offices operated for decades in many towns, now only represented by lumps of foundation on desert floor, and abandoned buildings.

Just as the early miners learned in plumbing the veins of minerals out of rocky earth, luck plays a big role. Copper towns need something beyond what lies under the ground to survive.

Many of the communities that grew up around mines share some characteristics: the wide streets with their diagonal parking spaces in front of strips of stores and businesses, that are more often empty than full. The towns are usually in hill country, and traditional department and grocery stores no longer occupy their former Main Street buildings. Garden shops, health food stores, bed and breakfast outfits, and gift shops appealing to tourists fill the old storefronts. A new school, a Target or Home Depot that may appear on the edge of town, and a tenacious optimism characterizes the former mining magnets that supported hundreds of families in their heyday. You find it all across Bisbee, Globe, Superior, Hayden, San Manuel, Clifton-Morenci, and Douglas.

BISBEE

Bisbee varies somewhat from this pattern because of geography. Swaddled in a gulch in the Mule Mountains of Southern Arizona, an old prospector named George Warren partnered with an Army scout to establish a claim in the 1870's. But Warren's propensity for drink and betting lost him the claim. In a classic story of Arizona's economy, investors from out of state purchased the Copper Queen mine in 1880. Judge DeWitt Bisbee never did actually visit the town that bears his name, but profited from the early extractions of what ended up being more than eight million tons of rich copper ore Bisbee mines yielded over the years. Phelps Dodge moved in near the Copper Queen, expanding the Lavender Pit mine which finally dried up in the 1970's. Several thousand miles of underground passageways still meander through the area today.

Mining may be a thing of the past, but the stories remain. A dark chapter in Arizona history played out in Bisbee in 1917 when union organizers for the International Workers of the World, called "Wobblies," began agitating for the thousands of mine workers to join the I.W.W. Phelps Dodge waged a fierce campaign against it, first using the newspapers the company owned. When that wasn't enough, several thousand Phelps Dodge supporters with white handkerchiefs tied around their sleeves, and carrying weapons, rounded up about as many I.W.W. agitators and supporters and forced them onto boxcars that dumped them in Columbus, New Mexico. While only two died, the incident illustrated the total dominion mining companies exercised over the people who worked for them, and the Bisbee Deportation became a symbol of the powerlessness of mineworkers everywhere.

Today all that remains of those workers and their powerful bosses are their homes: rustic colorful cottages on the lower slopes of Bisbee, and the elegant old Victorians built for the managers above. Class lines are being rejuvenated as the old homes are bought and restored.

Bisbee now has an unusual luxury for a small town: it is populated almost entirely by recently arrived residents. Many smaller communities are made up of residents born there or were moved there by parents or spouses. Homes in Bisbee have been enthusiastically purchased by transplants from far and near, brought by word of mouth or the odd travel article, and now residents embrace their home as the iconoclastic disparate society it is.

Christine Rhodes is one of the few who were brought as a child. "I'm definitely not a good example of what Bisbee is today," she says, "since I'm probably only one of twenty residents who hasn't chosen to live here. But none of us consider moving. Kids in my family who could have jobs elsewhere paying much more love it here, and would never talk about leaving." She refers to the Mule Mountain Pass that frames the entrance to Bisbee as "The Time Tunnel." "As soon as you come through it, things move at a slower pace."

Since mining has ended, the air is clean and clear. Crime rarely occurs; people nod and smile as they pass. Galleries and restaurants jostle for space on the winding streets with their boarding houses and small businesses. The architecture is a mix of Craftsman, Victorian, Territorial and others without any recognizable style, all now the beneficiaries of paint and patient hard work that is clearly bringing new life to the old buildings.

Bright wooden signs swing over the sidewalks with whimsical names proclaiming the merchandise inside. A bookstore with wooden floors offers everything from local history to tarot and witchcraft, as well as organic cotton clothing. Nearby, a candle shop is staffed by a woman who says she, together with half of Marin County, moved to Bisbee because Marin became overrun with wealthy city people. While this has driven up property values since the original (earnest hippies discovered the town in the 1970's and bought homes for mere hundreds of dollars) she raves about the community's volunteer efforts and generous support of various causes.

This is borne out by the announcements on bulletin boards of benefit concerts and town meetings. An open-air coffee shop hums with conversation as residents, tourists, and well-behaved dogs bask in the thin winter sunshine. An air of relaxation, conviviality and ease carries up the street to the Copper Queen Hotel, which has lodged dignitaries and tourists for more than a century. While its most popular room is said to be the one where John Wayne slept, the lobby and bar attract the most patrons. In the two minutes it takes to buy a cup of coffee, a customer is drawn into lighthearted banter that draws no distinctions between who lives here and who is visiting.

Bisbee may not be for everyone. While nightlife and community events are in abundance, its residents are an eclectic and freethinking group. While the population has fallen from about 20,000 in its heyday to about 6,000 today, the change in its inhabitants from being mostly miners to today's individuals tailoring their ideal lives, gives meaning to the concept of quality, not quantity.

GLOBE

Driving down the streets of Globe, Arizona, you see another former copper town trying to figure out a second act as a tourist attraction, with less certainty and direction. Although lacking the picturesque canyons and colorful homes on lopsided levels up the slopes of Bisbee, Globe residents would say their future requires the same characteristics admired in their founders: grit, pluck and hope.

If its early residents hadn't possessed a good helping of those qualities, the town would undoubtedly be tilting timbers and tumbleweed tracks today. In a state with an ample share of colorful Old West lore, Globe's raucous history still draws attention. Beginning in the Centennial Year, 1876, Globe City coped with gunfights, holdups, feuds, attacks, and hangings more briskly than most frontier towns. (Arizonan's last legal hanging was in Globe in 1936.) Some dustups involved famous characters.

Pearl Hart, who received national attention as a feisty outlaw in a field that was strictly male-dominated, began her criminal career in Globe in 1899. She and a companion, Joe Boot, decided to hold up the town stage after Pearl got word her mother was sick and needed her daughter. The plan was to finance the trip at other travelers' expense. Caught by local lawmen, she was sentenced to prison and taken to the Pima County jail, where a guard helped her escape. Later recaptured and sentenced to harsher holdings, Pearl Hart became something of a media sensation in the Yuma Territorial Prison. There reporters from eastern cities would come to interview the outspoken woman about her life. (Interestingly, her last residence ended up where she began her outlaw days: cells from the old Yuma Prison were transferred to the Globe Sheriff's Office.)

Another character out of the Old West magazines who had ties to Globe was one of the notorious Clanton brothers, famous for his participation in the gunfight at Tombstone's OK Corral. Phineas Clanton arrived in Globe after the gunfight, where he settled into the more prosaic profession of raising goats and married a widow. Eventually daily life accomplished what Wyatt Earp did not: Clanton died when a wagon rolled over on him.

Globe residents point with pride to other, more laudable locals. One was George W. P. Hunt, who famously served as Arizona's governor for six terms. Before entering government, it is said the teenage George made pocket money waiting tables in a local saloon.

A "Globe Girl Who Made Good" is Rose Mofford, who first assumed the position of Arizona Secretary of State before becoming famous as its first female governor. Sworn in after the impeachment of governor Evan Mecham brought unfortunate national attention, Mofford, better known as Rose to all, held the state together during shaky days in the 1980's. Her distinctive sugar-white beehive hairdo and comfortable graciousness were reassuring to a wounded and jumpy electorate. Declining to run again, Governor Mofford is remembered as a kind of Florence Nightingale, bringing civility and calm to a chaotic atmosphere.

Despite its central location, Globe was very much off the beaten path from its earliest days until the 1920's when Highway 60 was constructed. This cut the travel time from the mining town to Phoenix from two days to one.

Globe citizens, while they may not always agree, have learned the fine art of negotiation and compromise. Some point to the old story about how, after the schoolhouse was built, zealous leading lights discovered that the rule of having a brothel at least 400 feet away from a school had been violated. Careful measuring showed the distance to be four feet short. The madam responded to demands; she closed her doors with the promise that she would let no illegal activity occur within the first four feet of her front parlor.

Today, instead of such enterprises, the Adobe Ranch spa in Globe offers meditation, massage and healing treatments. Some businesses try to make up for the paucity of choices: Joe's Bar and Grill has "Mexican Food" on one window, "American Food" on the next, and "Italian Food" on the third. Globe residents seem to take a mournful pride in being the town in which J. C. Penney's closed its last store at the end of its catalogue empire.

While the median income of Globe's 7,000 or so souls is lower than the state's average, housing costs are also noticeably modest. Some enterprising residents are shrewdly purchasing old buildings and tracts of land, counting on Globe to emerge as a getaway for weary Valley residents seeking cool nights, quiet days and the solace of outdoor sports and recreation.

Kip Culver is the kind of person Globe can look to with hope. Saying he "didn't arrive by choice, but by stork," Kip spends his life helping Globe become the attraction residents visualize.

As a gateway for tourists, Globe has what Kip thinks is a unique draw: high desert with tall saguaros in one direction, lofty pines in another, and a lake for fishing and boating in a third. He says the people are as diverse as the landscape. "So many ethnic communities are here that we are all one town," he says. "There's no separation. And the uniqueness and the spirit of people here is genuine." In charge of the Cobre Valley Center for the Arts and the Globe Historic Main Street Program, Kip has the youth and vigor needed for the long haul, combined with an appreciation for his hometown that often doesn't come until later in life.

He says he was an anomaly in high school when most of the students' discussions centered on how fast graduates would be able to get out of town. "I was never at odds with it. It was my town," he says. "I've lived in Los Angeles, the Valley, Washington D.C., and traveled a great deal. I guess those things gave me an added appreciation for the idea that 'Home is Good.' "

At the cost of one dollar a year, the Main Street Program rents the former Gila County courthouse from the City as headquarters for the Cobre Valley Center for the Arts. Built in 1905, the courthouse had been abandoned, windows were broken, and pigeons had moved in. An imposing structure in classical style, the old courthouse is getting refurbished by the staff and volunteers, with a theater upstairs and gallery space on the middle floor. Leading visitors through the halls, Kip shows what the group has been up against: the original wainscoting covered by fiberboard partitions, spacious rooms broken into warrens, and years of dust and accumulated debris. The finished areas demonstrate the worth of their good efforts.

With his infectious charm and easy personality, Kip is an invitation to Globe personified. Hearing him talk about friends getting together on weekends creates wistful visions of belonging to such a community. Kip isn't afraid the town will become a sprawling and impersonal metropolis because the terrain itself will prevent it. From the hill overlooking the town, the steep and changing grades show clearly that this is not a place for developers to grade a few acres and put in cookie-cutter ranch homes.

As editor and publisher of the local Copper Country News, Rita Hassard agrees with Kip that new blood is vital to the town, but that the flavor of the community doesn't need changing. "It's hard sometimes to fit all the community news in the paper," she says. And while occasionally someone sends a vitriolic letter to the editor, most are enthusiastic. "A lot of time people will write in about how wonderful the police department is, how helpful the fire department is. People want to talk about the really great things they see here."

Mayor Paul Lucano says to him Globe's strength lies in its Mexican food. "You can't find the taste quite like it anywhere else," he says. Lucano is a hometown boy who retired from smelter work and came home. Having circled the globe many times, the Globe he wanted was this one. The gradual closing of the big mining operations meant having to think creatively about keeping the town alive, and as mayor, Lucano looks for options. One advantage Globe offers businesses, he says, is a stable water table. In a drought-ridden state with increasing limitations on water use, this is no small thing.

If residents can issue the right invitation to bring people to check out their town, they are confident the charms of Globe will shine brightly enough to bring new neighbors who want to stay.

MIAMI

Debbie Metz is a transplant from Anchorage, Alaska. "These mountains drew me here," she says. "We raised our family in Phoenix, but wanted to retire in a cottage with a picket fence." She gravitated to the nearby town of Miami, which is bordered by mines on three sides, and therefore not destined to grow too much beyond several thousand people. She doesn't find the slag tailings at all unattractive. "I'm proud of Arizona's heritage," she says. Copper is still big business here in Miami: seven million pounds were shipped worldwide last year. "And since my mother has property in Jerome and Bisbee, I'm a mining town junkie."

Metz is in charge of the Miami Home Tour, and wants young families and retirees from the Valley who are looking for a vintage home to know that the deals are to be found here. "We have the century-old two-bedroom cottages with glass doorknobs," she says. "And you can't beat the prices. Or the weather. The sky is bluer here than any place in the state."

HAYDEN

Some copper towns have a harder time flourishing now that their heyday has passed. While less than 40 miles separate the town of Globe from Hayden, the two mining towns have traveled different paths since copper ceased to support them.

Hayden was a company town created in 1910, and at one time boasted a main street bustling with businesses. Working in a company town meant living in houses owned by Phelps Dodge, so when you quit or retired, you moved. Sharing a border with Winkelman on the Gila River, Hayden occupies three distinct hills: Mill side in the center held the mill and businesses, Smelter side the mine, and San Pedro the Hispanic population of the typically segregated mining community.

Even among those who love their hometown fiercely, Hayden looks like a ghost town of the future. The population has fallen from several thousand in its heyday to about 800, and is still dropping.

Pete and Joe Rios were the 12th and 13th of fourteen "copper children" from Hayden. Today Pete Rios is a longtime successful state senator for his hometown district, and Joe his chief of staff. The two care passionately about the youth of their area, and talk easily about the economics and school districts of Hayden-Winkelman.

Growing up, they loved the weekly baseball games, playing by the river, and the closeness of the community. But when the livelihood of virtually every family depended on copper, there were consequences. The Rios brothers tell of breathing searing fumes from the Kennecott copper processing and knowing that fresh air would mean economic catastrophe for the families there.

"It was hard to run laps in PE in school," says Pete. "The sulphuric acid in the air made it hard to breathe. But a lot of people were willing to put up with it, because it meant all the jobs." He said it was years before residents addressed contaminated water supplies out of fear of jeopardizing their livelihood. "You'd rather have a place you can live and work than die a slow death."

"I kind of blame the company," says Joe, "because in the 70's they made 500 million dollars profit, and they didn't invest it in the town, cleaning up and installing equipment."

After serving in Vietnam, Joe returned to mine work, and was instrumental in bringing union support to the employees. He says in those days, the men worked together, hunted together and knew a rare camaraderie that is hard to find in larger cities that lack the common employee of the old mining towns. "You were just always together," he says. "I've seen it all change. Now, if you're going to work, you have to leave."

Pete agrees. He says the town is now largely populated by retirees, who can depend on a pension rather than a paycheck. However, that creates its own problems. "It used to be everyone supported what the schools wanted," he says, "because everyone's children went there. But now, the retirees refuse to support the bond issues."

In fact, the schools were in danger of being shut down after poor financial forecasting almost bankrupted the system. The Rios brothers worked long hours with the legislative process to restructure the debt and keep the classrooms open.

Their own children have moved because of the lack of jobs. Joe laughs, happily describing a Thanksgiving weekend, seeing the neighborhood streets choked with cars as children and grandchildren came home to visit. "There will be hundreds of people, just on two streets. You look at all those people, and think of all the votes we could get," he says, "if there were just jobs for them."

But even as much as they love their childhood memories, and as connected as they are to state government and its resources, the Rios brothers don't have any magic waiting in the wings for Hayden. "The problem is the area never diversified," says Pete. "When the mine suffered, everything suffered. The hospital closed, the businesses left, and now it keeps going downhill."

Joe describes seeing the businesses boarded up as a sad inevitability. "It's closer to a ghost town than a community," he says. "The problem is, we're so far removed. All the copper towns in the area get together to see if there's anything we can do to try to attract people. But it's just not a good location." He adds sadly, "Even the rivers have mostly run dry."

But if the town is dying, the Rios brothers are not nostalgic for every aspect of it. While the young people all played together ("Even if we fought, it wasn't about race," says Pete), segregation was alive and well among adults. Joe recounts finding a baseball glove he had borrowed and going to return it to his friend. "His mother, she just took it from me without saying anything, using two fingers as if it were dirty from me," he says. "I can still remember the look I got."

Copper gave Arizona thousands of jobs, and earned plenty of money for the companies that ran the mines. But in the classic tale of boom and bust, the era has ended. Some towns will survive. Others will join the dozens of ghost towns already scattered across the state, offering tourists with four-wheel drive vehicles and cameras tantalizing glimpses of times gone by – a crumbled adobe building, rusting wheel rims, perhaps a cemetery is all that remains. Which Arizona mining towns will manage to avoid ghost town status is still a story being played out, long after the veins of ore already have.

KIP CULVER

DOUGLAS DOORWAY

GLOBE VISTA

BOYS AT PARADE

CHAPTER 11

SIERRA VISTA AND ARIZONA BASES: MILITARY MEETS MAINSTREAM

Soldiers have been part of Arizona since the mid-1800's, when scouts and battalions were dispatched to the unknown West to protect settlers against local Indian tribes not willing to relinquish their lands and lifestyle. At one time more than fifty forts dotted the rudimentary maps of the Arizona Territory.

After years of supporting U.S. troops who were fighting or chasing Geronimo, the famous Apache Chief and renegade, Fort Apache, north of Globe, fell into ruin. As tensions between settlers and tribes lessened, many of the forts became redundant. Fort Whipple, near Prescott, was abandoned after fifty years of action, including serving as General George Crook's headquarters in the 1880's. (The redoubtable General Crook, known as the Army's greatest Indian fighter and remembered for the respect and regard he held for the native tribes, served at many of Arizona's bases during the 1870's and 1880's.) Fort Defiance, which billeted soldiers fighting the Navajo, ironically became the offices of the Bureau of Indian Affairs after it was decommissioned. In fact, Forts Mohave, Yuma, Verde and McDowell all became incorporated within Indian reservations.

Some forts stayed active because troubles with Mexico lingered after most of the tribes were relegated to reservations. Pancho Villa continued to be a thorn in the US Army's side into the 20th century. Fort Grant near Safford – and therefore close to the borderlands – was last used as a troops transfer station for Rough Riders during the Spanish American War in the early 1900's. But all of the dozens of Army installations were eventually shut down, with the exception of Fort Huachuca.

Why did Fort Huachuca alone remain a functioning fort, when Forts Grant, Bowie and Buchanan nearby closed? Part of the answer lies with what is now Sierra Vista, which became its support community, which the other forts lacked. From its early days Sierra Vista underwent a long series of colorful titles from its first days. One of its first names was Garden Canyon, because the troops at the fort were supplied with local produce by the citizens there. It was also called Campstone, Fry, Turner and Overton. The name Sierra Vista was not official until 1955. The community and the fort began symbiotic, and the role remains today.

While Fort Huachuca is the only Army installation in the state, Arizona has a huge military presence. Between Luke Air Force Base near Mesa, Davis Monthan in Tucson, the Arizona National Guard's Camp Navajo by Flagstaff, the Yuma Proving Ground, Barry M. Goldwater Range Complex (all Air Force) and the Yuma Marine Air Corps, both active duty personnel and retired military make up a sizable percentage of our Arizona residents, as well as our economy. Estimates are that more than $50 million annually enters the state from Davis Monthan payroll alone. More than 40,000 retired military receive pensions of more than $1.5 billion annually. All in all, the estimated yearly figures for military money in the state comes to $5.5 billion.

This explains in large part why Arizona fights to keep all its bases open. Tucson made what some residents see as a deal with mixed benefits in 2004, extending hours and flight paths for the military jets flying over Tucson to and from Davis Monthan. While they don't enjoy the nighttime noise and uneasily fear a crash like one in the early 1980's that occurred on a main street in midtown, Tucsonans realize the economic benefits of the base are huge.

Aside from the retirees who still shop on base, some Tucsonans have no more than a vague awareness of its existence. Old-timers remember whispers during the Cold War that Tucson would be a prime Communist target because of Davis Monthan, and for years Saturday noon was marked by testing of the Early-Warning System, more commonly known as War-Horns, reminding the population that peace was touchy and uncertain. But unless you drive south on Alvernon to look at the rusty vestiges of all manner of aircraft parked in rows, or attend an event at the Officers Club, military and mainstream rarely mix.

This is in contrast to Sierra Vista, which regards Fort Huachuca as part of its community. The town and the base are seamless; cross a main street and you are on the Fort property. The buildings have retained their frontier flavor, low and trimmed in white. There is a rustic impression that may fly in the face of modern military life, but fits perfectly in a western town.

Bob and Jackie Dorr moved here from Sonoita in large part because of the fort. Being retired military, they were instantly comfortable. "Sonoita was beautiful, but shopping and medical care were very inconvenient," says Jackie. "Here we have all that, and we're attached to the fort. It's like our own playground."

Bob smiles, "We feel like we belong." He adds that besides shopping and dining out, they love Fort Huachuca for the recreation. "It's a whole other world, the canyons we hike on the fort. Huge trees, turkey, mountain lion, bear. Today we saw four deer."

Tucson would have been the logical place to retire, he says, because he was last stationed at Davis Monthan, and family lives there. "But this was it from the moment we saw it. The fort has such a history, buildings that were constructed in the 1880's are still being used."

Because he's lived on base in other cities, Bob knows that generally military personnel doesn't mix much with townsfolk. He was delighted to find Fort Huachuca the exception. "This post and the town work together, the best of any I've seen. If there's a circus on the fort, the town is invited. The golf course is open to the public. And the hunting area is for general use."

Christine Rhodes' grandfather was a member of the famed Buffalo Soldiers, first in South Dakota, then at Fort Huachuca. Her family has stayed in the area. Although she is no longer part of a military family, she says she's often at the fort. "Weddings, birthday parties – events not at all connected to the military. Lots of groups have meetings here. Before 9/11, you didn't even have to sign in."

Fort Huachuca is by far the largest employer in town, and city council officials work to make sure Congress knows the military is supported by Sierra Vista.

"It's good the town depends on it," says Bob. "They get along so well."

So well, in fact, that when July Kelley had the choice of going home to family in Texas when her husband was transferred overseas, or staying in Sierra Vista, she chose to stay. "It just felt like a good community," she says. "I really like the people here." Taking classes at Cochise College has drawn her into relationship with people off post, and she has became involved in local politics. "As a military child, you crave deeper connections," she says. "Now I'm so glad my husband was stationed here. We have three years more, and I've met all these great people." July could be speaking for Sierra Vista itself when she says it might be a lack of connections that makes residents reach out naturally.

Alice Joiner says when she came to Sierra Vista thinking about buying a home, the hospitality was astonishing." I've never met so many friendly people. I couldn't find a place to do email, and the woman at the Chamber of Commerce said, 'If I hadn't taken my lunch already I'd take you home and you could use mine.' But she directed me to the cyber café, and they didn't even make me buy a cup of coffee!"

She has found what she called "belongingness" in the senior groups and retired military here.

While most Arizona host cities value their military bases, not all are as compatable. Luke AFB in western Maricopa County is one of the key bases for the training of F-16 fighter pilots. It is indispensible to our national defense. That is why fighting for its continued existance in the face of a national wave of base closings is a required article of faith among Arizona politicians.

A sign in the visitors' center boasts: "Welcome to the largest fighter training base in the world." Valley resident Jim Carter, who served here after a tour of Vietnam in '65 and retired as an Air Force captain, said the best thing about Arizona is the weather.

"Due to our climate, you have a whale of a production line for pilots," he said, "because you don't lose any time to rain."

Unlike Fort Huachuca, Luke Air Force Base is tightly closed to civilians. Approach the Main Gate, and without a military ID you will be asked to leave with little patience or humor. Also unlike Fort Huachuca, Luke has few neighbors. Despite the fact that it occupies the fast-growing West Valley, Luke is bordered mostly by vacant land.

But even though the base doesn't welcome civilians, residents of Glendale and Peoria are fiercely loyal to Luke. On any given day, if you drive across Northern, which is also the northern boundary of the base, cars are parked randomly along the street, between "No Parking" signs. This is where enthusiats come to watch the fighter pilots train. They can point out to a newcomer the best place to stand for each runway approach.

"If you're right over here," says Dave Drown, a retireee out with a couple of friends, "they come in about fifty feet over your head. You can see the whites of their eyes. If you wave, they usually wave back."

Drown isn't retired Air Force — he was in the Army — but he comes out from Sun City Grand about once a week. "I just love planes," he says. He adds that the wide swaths of empty land around the base are mostly privately owned, which the Luke Air Force Base Public Affairs office confirms. Drown worries that the price of real estate will erode the buffer zone and cause the pilots problems. But the Public Affairs office statement is that laws prohibit development that would interfere with runway and landing patterns. As the city swells around the cushion, it seems possible that eventually high-powered real estate could possibly prevail. And the risks to Luke are enormous. If flight operations are reduced, the base — while invaluable to Arizona's economy — loses relative value in the intense competition for Pentagon resources, and could even face the threat of closure in a future round of base closings that are required by Federal law.

Even without being allowed on base, civilians can feel included. Drown says he's played golf at Falcon Dunes, the course just behind the base, with his Air Force brother-in-law. Just after he speaks, an enlisted man in uniform walks past, carrying his clubs. Drown watches. "I wonder if he'll even use a caddy," he says. "With pins like that, he doesn't need to."

After scanning the skies and listening, Drown and his companions decide the morning training session is probably over. (They can usually guage the morning and afternoon sessions winding down by watching where the planes taxi.) They seem reluctant to call it a day, asking a young man with a huge camera if he's ever taken pictures at the Gila Range, and how close you might be able to get. While the Public Affairs office says parking there is prohibitied, no personnel came out to chase spectators away. Maybe the Air Force understands the romance of watching the fighter planes swoop and circle overhead. maybe the community goodwill is worth keeping an eye on the people — mostly men — gathered on the shoulder of the road, with cameras and binoculars and dreams, watching the young pilots soar, and land, at Luke Air Force Base.

LAKE HAVASU BAY

CHAPTER 12

"WE MADE IT!"
THE PIONEERS OF LAKE HAVASU CITY

You've got to hand it to Robert McCullough for vision. Most people looking at the land where Lake Havasu City now watches the Colorado River from the shore didn't see what he did in the early 1960's. Only McCullough, who tested the outboard motors his company manufactured here, saw the future site of a grand world-class tourist icon. He wisely invited Disneyland designer C.V. Wood to join him on his quest.

Somewhere between apocryphal and attributed, the story goes that McCullough first approached Italian dignitaries about purchasing the Leaning Tower of Pisa. Upon being refused, he heard about how the London Bridge was slowly sinking upon its piles into the Thames, and he snapped it up for a tad less than 2.5 million dollars. However, McCullough ended up shelling out twice that amount to get the 10,000-plus granite blocks taken apart, painstakingly labeled, shipped to Long Beach and trucked to the future site at Lake Havasu City. The blocks were reassembled and ready to be crossed in 1964 – although at first there was no water replacing the Thames. McCullough got a channel dredged, creating a basin on the Colorado. The bridge, which had originally been dedicated in London in 1831, received a proper dedication from the kindly Lord Mayor of London, who crossed the Atlantic to preside at this second grand opening of the London Bridge.

Now the bridge has a different look. At the Lake Havasu Museum of History, you can see one of the blocks as it looked in London; a deep, gummy, tar hew, stained by more than a century of coal pollution. Once here, the mixture of sand, heat, water and wind scrubbed the granite from sooty black to a gentle beige. The London Bridge gained a new lease on life in its retirement to the desert, as have many of the ardent residents who followed.

Some of the first to call Lake Havasu home were flown in on eleven planes taken from McCullough's own fleet. Quaintly called "Holly Dolly Flights," the name was taken from McCullough's wife Holly.

In the 1960's, men hired for their fresh engaging style and ability to talk their way into living rooms in major cities all over the East and Midwest, would bring with them a small portable Dukane slide projector and heavy black LP albums. After creating an instant theater that brought the sights and sounds of Lake Havasu to snowy climes, the salesman would offer the prospects a free chance to come and visit the community-to-be.

Jim Hoffman was one who said "yes" to the invitation. "I didn't really have to be convinced," says the former Michigan resident. "I recognized when I got here that it was the best opportunity, best financial decision I would ever make in my life."

Before he could retire full time, Hoffman had to continue to commute between Detroit and Lake Havasu for six years. But he loves being one of the people who made it – and made Lake Havasu City a reality.

Bob and Bea Klief exemplified the reaction of many of the original residents. Bob says he was "tired of shoveling snow" in Wisconsin, and saw chance to be a new settler, heading West for a new life. But Bea said she didn't want to be a settler. "We were put up in a hotel, and we were rarely allowed to leave, except with a salesman. Asked if she could see the vision, she says emphatically, "No. No, siree. Not here."

Part of the reason was that no one ready to break ground on the raw new home sites had experience building the split-level style of Bea's dream home. But free flight and marketing did its work. They bought a home and started a bicycle and tire business. Semi-retired, they got to watch the desert blossom like a rose.

Which was not a comfortable process for all of the new residents.

"It was so quiet, it made your head hurt," recalls Ophelia Toth. She was surprised one evening back in Detroit when her husband told her company was coming for dinner – and it turned out to be one of the eager salesmen. "He went through his spiel," she says, "and I asked if he'd ever been there. He confessed, 'Well, no, ma'am, I haven't.' But we decided to take the trip out anyway, for an adventure. It was a big thing to leave our families, but we decided to buy.

"The first two years it was miserable. But we kind of grew into the surroundings, and got to know people, then started liking it."

Now, 32 years later, Ophelia can't think of any other place she'd like to live, although she adds with a smile that "there are a few places I wouldn't mind going during the summer."

Kathy Cox, who moved from Denver, admits to "a love-hate relationship" with Lake Havasu beginning with her husband's first job interview in Lake Havasu back in 1975.

"I remember in the 60's picking up a magazine and reading about a man moving the London Bridge to the Arizona desert," relates the lively blonde. "It was about the same time that Roy Rogers stuffed Trigger. I thought, 'Here we go, one more Disneyland kind of thing!' But when my husband got the job interview, I didn't associate it with the magazine article I'd read ten years earlier. When we got off the plane, he looked around and muttered, 'No way! We'll take the next plane back.' I convinced him to at least stay for the interview. Turns out it took place in a metal trailer. But it was the only interview, and the only job offer, he got."

Cox laughs remembering the trip across Arizona with 13 cats in the station wagon. "I loved Flagstaff," she continued. "Then we turned off Interstate 40 onto I-95, and had to stop for burros. Then it was 120 degrees when we finally arrived in town. No one could afford air conditioning. It was hot in the new house. It was hot outside. It was hot in the car. There was no cold water for showers. There were times I thought Lake Havasu wasn't going to make it. There were times I thought I wasn't going to make it."

But the formula for settling into any new community began to work.

"You make friends; you develop a sense of community. We all had common experiences. My grandmother had moved in the 1890's and been part of creating a new town. I'd always thought that would be incredible. And we got to do it."

Arizona has always been a place for people to start over – to tame the wild places, to create a home, a town. But it's hard to look at Lake Havasu City and not see what was there before – because there still seems to be plenty of empty, hot, dry land on either side of the town.

Lake Havasu, itself, was formed with the construction of Parker Dam on the Colorado River. Pittsburgh Point, a finger of land reaching into the lake, caught McCullough's eye, and he bought thousands of acres around that area. After London Bridge was reconstructed, McCullough had a trench dredged out, severing Pittsburgh Point and turning it into an island that can be reached by crossing the bridge. Campgrounds, hotels, restaurants, and shops share space on the island across the water from the main part of the city.

If there is a downtown, it's the English Village next to London Bridge. You can see C.V. Wood's influence here, since the bright beds crowded with seasonal flowers, half-timbered buildings, and bright red British phone booths could come from an area in Disneyland. Large lions spittling into the spray ring a wide circular fountain. The London Bridge Resort boasts the only replica of the Royal Carriage used in Queen Victoria's coronation. Close to the water are the quaint storefronts where browsers can buy anything from little double-decker buses to shirts with beer logos and shell anklets. The United Kingdom meets Spring Break here.

Just as you'd have completely different personalities in a group of fifty people, each community in Arizona has its own fingerprint, pulse and identity. Because our state grows at such a rate, some communities are brand new babies, completely captivating. Other towns struggle with adolescence, becoming something new. Some are full of concerned citizens forming committees, meeting to shake their heads about schisms between growth and no-growth groups, worried about apathy and fanaticism alike. But here in Lake Havasu City there is no such encounter group venting. Lake Havasu is the boy who seems to regard life as an opportunity to learn, share and have fun every day. People here like their lives. Which makes sense – they have chosen them.

For one thing, it's hard to worry about growth when land is so accessible in all directions. It's hard to worry too much about water when it's so visible from almost all over town. And everyone here is a relative newcomer, so you don't have the same sense of old families being encroached upon as some places in Arizona do.

Lake Havasu City has come a long way since the first homebuyers could look across empty land and point to a square on the map representing where their new home would begin to rise. About fifty thousand people live here on the land sloping down to the river (although the terrain is so hilly that it averages out to be about 500 feet above sea level). Two hours from Vegas, three from Phoenix, to residents it is near all the amenities without having to put up with the populations, the traffic and the distractions of the larger cities.

Residents agree that one of the biggest problems newcomers face is not understanding that coyotes are desert animals that will consume small prey such as housecats. Other than that, the newcomers are carefree. They love the colors of the mountains stretching away from the lake; they share the satisfaction of seeing the town expand and attract new residents. They share the nod of people who recognize a job well done to which they have contributed. By being willing to walk away from their established home somewhere else and come to the water's edge, they have experienced the settler's triumph of creating a home in the wilderness. They laugh fondly about moving here in the winter and not finding out until summer that there was no cold water in the pipes during the hot season. They remember with fondness the days before home mail delivery, which succeeded in bringing people together as they met at the post office. Now, as a payoff for taking the chance on a Holly Dolly flight, the early residents themselves are the settlers.

"We made it!" one says, and everyone laughs in agreement. In a world where most things are made for us, prepackaged and distributed, it's a sweet feeling to look around and know that you contribute to creating a community like this from the ground up, or in this case, perhaps, from the water up. They laugh again talking about Lake Havasu City having something in common with Moscow: getting the first McDonald's meant culture had finally arrived. Despite the coyotes, despite the heat, despite the tourists, Lake Havasu City is a fine home.

"A lot of settlers just followed their men whether they liked it or not," says Val Johnson. "But I wanted to come. I liked the wildness."

That wildness initially meant no grocery store. Val and her neighbors would take long grocery lists for other women when they went into Kingman or Las Vegas. The Foodland opening in 1972 solved that problem. Now, besides grocery mega-stores, Home Depot, Wal-Mart, Pizza Hut and Taco Bell occupy less prime real estate. You can still find places in town that won't take checks, but you can also find the ubiquitous ATM's to solve the problem. Residents take the vacationers and visitors with a grain of salt, as they have to anywhere that most of the world regards as a vacation spot. The traffic, the crowding during holiday weekends, the pushy tourists take their lumps when locals are asked about the city's problems.

Regan Ross is a first-generation Lake Havasu City resident. In her mid-twenties, she is younger than the town.

"It's hard," she says, "because there aren't many people here in my age group – career-minded and in their 20's." She laughs wryly when someone mentions the sign promising "mall soon!" on a plat of land that has made this promise for nine years. Unless you live for water sports, Lake Havasu City is not a mecca for young professionals. But John Masden, who came from Kansas City with his parents, sees that changing.

"I think the age range will fill in," he says. "It's a matter of time. I see a lot of the same things occurring that happened when I was young: school budget overrides fail; apathy kills education projects. But now both old and new people are stepping up to the plate; a K-12 education foundation has been started."

If you go to the Lake Havasu Museum of History, a docent sitting behind the desk will escort you through the displays, which begin with a look at the Chemehuevi tribe, part of the Mojave people. Dioramas show how they lived, the pottery they made, and the tools they used. Anglo history begins in what is now Lake Havasu City when gold was discovered in the Parker area in 1857. Steamboat landings sprung up along the river with names like Aubrey City, Port Famine and Isabell. The Parker Dam is the deepest in the world, the museum display says, like an iceberg with 75 percent of the structure underwater. McCullough figures prominently in the museum's materials, including a photo of the man golfing with President Dwight W. Eisenhower, a prototype of a plane McCullough designed that never got off the ground, and a pair of the saddle oxfords McCullough always wore, autographed by those involved in bringing London Bridge to Lake Havasu. It is appropriate that he is such an integral part of the displays. Few towns can look so completely to one man for their genesis.

McCullough would surely be proud to see Lake Havasu flourishing, and maybe even more pleased at the pleasure and pride the residents take in their community.

"There are still enough people you know in the community. You run into someone on a daily basis," says John Madsden.

And Kathy Cox, with her professed love-hate relationship with Lake Havasu City, breaks off mid-sentence to point across the water.

"Look at that; I love that," she says of the view. "Purple mountains majesty. I was asked to help with a brochure for tourists when I first moved here, and came up with 'There's no place like it,' figuring at least people wouldn't see my irony. But now, it's true in the best way." She looks fondly at the scene, just one of the satisfied residents who made Lake Havasu what it is.

LAKE HAVASU BEACH

WEATHERFORD HOTEL

HERITAGE SQUARE

CHAPTER 13

FLAGSTAFF:
PEAKS AND VALLEYS

The town of Flagstaff nestles at the base of the San Francisco Peaks like a contented pet lies at its master's feet. First a logging community, now a haven for environmentalists, wilderness lovers, scholars, astronomers and even golfers, Flagstaff is both beautiful and blemished, depending on the season, the neighborhood and the light.

Surrounded by the largest forest of ponderosa pine in the continental United States, Flagstaff seems rustic and alpine. Named for a ponderosa that served as a flagpole, or staff, for the Fourth of July centennial celebration in 1876, Flag Staff was two words until citizens of the sprawling mining camp voted it the official name in 1881. The construction of the Northern Arizona Normal School at the turn of the century showed that the town was more than merely lumberjacks.

Early photos preserved in the wonderful archives in the Northern Arizona University's special collections section of the library show raw, rough buildings, later replaced by the early familiar façade of downtown. But the San Francisco Peaks, benevolent silhouettes behind every era's version of Flagstaff, are changeless, except by season. The vivid gold of aspen are almost blinding when observed from the middle of a stand of quaking trees. Either lightly tipped or generously draped with snow in winter, or green and covered with familiar piles of afternoon clouds in summer, the peaks are the touchstone for anyone who loves Flagstaff.

By the 1950's, Flagstaff was primarily a college town, its teachers' college having proudly evolved into Arizona State College. It was a stop for tourists driving Route 66 in their spare time. Today it is a city of more than 50,000 souls, its college is now Northern Arizona University, and the town copes with fractionalizing and growth like other urban communities it seeks to avoid. Still, as a "Gateway to the Grand Canyon," Flagstaff can seem much smaller than its actual size.

Part of the reason may come from the fact that while Flagstaff is on the crossroads of Interstate 40 and Interstate 17, it has comparatively few exits from either. Many of the newer developments are visible only at their entrance, with the forest camouflaging the homes from the road. Near campus, it retains an eclectic, energetic, university feeling, as bicycles and golden retrievers share space with very fit people sipping coffee after a morning trail run. Rather than sprawl, Flagstaff has zones – the campus area, the ski area, the country club or the lakes, each with their reams of construction, but nowhere one giant wave of subdivisions spreading from a center strike zone.

After coming into town, go north and you cross the railroad tracks. One of Flagstaff's old-fashioned charms remains the trains passing through – some 90 a day. The gates swing down, traffic north and south stops, and the town is serenaded by the mighty tones of train whistles. Just north of the tracks, downtown invites pedestrians to stroll past organic restaurants to outdoor outfitters, to the post office or the bank, with earnest storefronts in grand old sandstone buildings. The restored Orpheum Theater has cushioned courting couples in its balcony since the 1930's. The historic Monte Vista and Weatherford Hotels both have rooms where Zane Grey wrote his famous western prose and there are bars where irascible writer Edward Abbey drank with his friends. Sidewalks are charmingly brick, and the scent of roasting coffee beans mixes with chili cooking. It is the downtown every city wishes it had.

If you drive along Butler Avenue, you cross the "maintenance yard" section of Flagstaff, with hardware stores, truck stops and motels scattered between parks and asphalt. Continue east and you come to new Flagstaff, where the mall and country club bring a more franchise generic feeling to the surroundings. Northeast toward Page, independent people have bought land without a lot of zoning to get in the way, and the outskirts are dotted with a variety of dwellings whose only constant is the vibrant changing-hued views of mountain and meadow, along with a shared connection to the peaks that provides the town's common emotional core.

If you go north from downtown instead, toward the Grand Canyon, Flagstaff's Museum of Northern Arizona and Snowbowl Ski Area beguile you into turning off the road and exploring. Flagstaff has a dozen looks and flavors. The homogenizing factors are that the landscape is breathtaking, and that more houses spring up all the time.

While lumber was Flagstaff's genesis, with the first mill opening in 1882, the city and its surrounding ponderosa forest have always had a tumultuous relationship. Three big mills had saws running by 1910, but after World War I a national depression closed them, and while one came back during the 20's, it was again shut down during the Great Depression in 1933. Southwest Lumber Mills started up in 1937, and by the 1950's Kaibab Lumber had enfolded the former Babbitt Mill. Eventually, however, it became clear in the 1980's that forests weren't regenerating fast enough to keep up with cutting, and the old growth trees were virtually gone.

The drought that began at the dawn of this millennium has been compounded by fires and an infestation of bark beetles. So while currently the Forest Service and the community struggle with how to make the forest sound, safe, and profitable, it is only the latest chapter in the uneasy dance between ponderosa and human. Early records show droughts closing lumber operations a century ago. Despite the green of forests, under the tall pines soil and stone are still often baked to dry dust. In the summer, the almost buttery scent of pine needles thick under sunny skies can be both intoxicating and worrisome. Flagstaff residents have always struggled with nature's cycles.

Richard Mangum, retired Superior Court Judge for Coconino County, has developed a reputation as a writer and historian since stepping down from the bench. He told once of a curse exchanged between early Mormon pioneers Brigham Young and John D. Lee, when the former turned the latter over to federal officials for his part in the tragic Mountain Meadow Massacre in Utah. Betrayed by his friend and trusted colleague, Lee apparently put a curse on Young, his children, and his children's children. Young returned the curse.

"We're still kind of waiting to see," Mangum reported wryly, "because a Young and a Lee fell in love, and I am a great-grandson of both of those men." So, steeped in northern Arizona lore, its no surprise Mangum developed an interest in the area. He and his wife, Sherry, can be seen strolling the streets of downtown Flagstaff in period dress, giving tours of the historic buildings and sharing lesser-known anecdotes about early citizens. As a boy, Mangum prowled the grounds of the old home Percival Lowell built near the observatory on Mars Hill. He remembers that Lowell's widow, heartbroken upon his death, would spend hours at the mausoleum that overlooked downtown Flagstaff as it was near the telescope where Lowell spent his nights scanning the skies for signs of a suspected ninth planet, and where his assistant, Clyde Tombaugh, later confirmed Pluto's existence. In their books, the Mangums preserve the feisty and freethinking pioneers whose spirit attracts similar personalities still.

Many legacies left by old families are still part of today's Flagstaff. The Riordan Mansion, now an Arizona State Park, lets us peer into the past preserved in the Craftsman mansion where the lumber magnate brothers, Timothy and Michael, raised their children. The Colton House, where archaeologist Harold Colton lived while doing important work documenting the lives of the Indian tribes in the area, is now a haven for seminars and retreats. John Wesley Powell's fearless descent into the Grand Canyon and exploration of the Colorado River is recalled when one enters Flagstaff from the south and crosses under J.W. Powell Boulevard.

Of course, the Babbitt name endures. The five brothers who came west in the 1880's began the dynasty, which has been involved in virtually every venture in Flagstaff. Still today, Jim Babbitt runs his outfitters' store on the ground floor of the restored Babbitt Building downtown. Bruce Babbitt expanded the family profile from representing Northern Arizona to representing the entire state when he was a successful two-term governor in the 1970's and 80's. He then took the name national by running for president in 1988, and serving as Secretary of the Interior under Bill Clinton. In Brothers Five, a biography of the Babbitts, Dean Smith writes that the family was always bold: C. J. Babbitt attempted to purchase the Bright Angel Trail leading into the Grand Canyon; Billy Babbitt took the unusual measure of employing a bodyguard during the range wars; John Babbitt served in the Arizona State Senate; and George Babbitt was mayor when he hosted the United States Congressional delegation that came out in 1905 to study whether statehood lay on Arizona's horizon. (That came to fruition seven years later.)

Anyone who is prosperous, political or prominent has detractors, and the generations of Babbitts who did business in ranching, mercantile, trading posts, autos, lumber and other ventures are no exception. But the Babbitts have dozens of admirers for every critic. Mangum, Riordan, Lowell, Babbitt – these are grand old names in Arizona.

Regardless of how many pioneer names can be found in the telephone directory, the real heritage shared by Flagstaff residents remains the San Francisco peaks. The town has stretched and grown under their benign watch. It is the distinctive outline of Mt. Humphreys and Agassiz, sloping down to a gentle trio of hills the Hopi called Baby Face for its resemblance to an infant's profile, that lets travelers know they are at home. You can see this outline from a long way off in any direction. Some feel instantly better in sight of the Peaks.

"I'm here because of the Peaks," says Ann Kirkpatrick, an attorney with a delicate face and clear eyes, who was recently elected to State Legislature. "As a child I fell in love with them, when we lived in Whiteriver and would go to Holbrook for community concerts and fairs. So when I was out of law school and working as a Pima County clerk, we received a call one day asking if any recent graduates were willing to work up here. I said yes, drove up the next day, and have been here ever since. I can have views of the Peaks from my home, and my office."

The Peaks transcend any political, ethnic and professional barriers," agrees Pam Hyde, who works on environmental issues in Flagstaff. She points out almost no one moves to Flagstaff for a job. They decide to move here first. "The job is the last piece in the puzzle."

But the "valleys" are also felt. Linda Hall, who is now retired, sympathizes with those trying to find work to support a family. "Here, it isn't a matter of being able to get a job," she says. "It's not being able to get enough jobs to stay."

Residents joke that there are more waitresses with masters' degrees in Flagstaff than anywhere else. Because you can ski, hike, row, rock climb, go caving, swimming and flying within an hour of Flagstaff, residents are less interested in the perfect profession than they are being able to support the leisure activities. Tourism is fairly steady, but the increasing number of hotels and restaurants sometimes seems to outpace the visitors. The most fortunate may be those who can have it both ways: live here, and work somewhere else.

"Doctors and lawyers can live in Phoenix, and travel up here to a second home," says Kirkpatrick. "They need the better jobs to pay student loans. People used to be willing to live at a lower economic level, but now Presidio in the Pines and Forest Highlands are mostly summer homes."

"The house behind me is a second home," says Hyde. "Most people buying up here live in Phoenix. It makes a difference. An elementary school is closing because of it. We're beginning to feel around the edges of what the impact could be."

Coconino County has the youngest average population in the state. The industries of tourism, education, astronomy and environmental leader W.L. Gore bring erudition without pollution to Flagstaff. So the only real physical challenge facing the town is growth. How many more people can the land, and its water, support? It depends on whom you ask. Developers submit 100-year plans; environmentalists whisper darkly these are based on bad science.

Kurt Davis and his wife Janet fall into that category. Now a consultant who works in Phoenix and Flagstaff, Davis says the couple had promised themselves before moving to Washington DC that they would someday return. After working in the federal government during the Reagan administration, and in Arizona in the attorney general's and the governor's office, Davis's appointment to on the Board of Regents led him to NAU. But it was more about lifestyle than profession.

"We had missed the beauty of green places," says Davis, a genial man who probably looked older when he was young and will look younger when he's old. "We missed the exhilaration of four seasons. Also, this is one of the few places in Arizona where you can see elk grazing as you drive from home to downtown.

Like any place, it could be hard to get into if your enjoyment is driven by being part of certain social circles," he says. "But through church, community organizations, NAU athletics and cultural opportunities, as well as children's activities, it's very easy to meet and build a wonderful circle of friends. Even politically, the inner circle is easy to enter, if your brain – and your mouth – are big enough."

Politics in the old days used to be closely managed by the few, the "old guard." But a community whose population is approaching six figures as Flagstaff's is, is much harder to rule with backroom deals and handshakes. To some, the process, now, works well.

In an office on the second floor of the Babbitt building, Rose Houk writes books and articles that often celebrate Flagstaff's rich history. Her surroundings are an author's dream; the original sandstone walls meet the patterned tin roof above her desk. From her deep chair she looks out on Heritage Square, the heart of downtown, with the familiar line of the Peaks in the background.

She speaks proudly of the creation of connective bike trails throughout the area, local support for "Big Box" ordinances to help small businesses, the Dark Sky Initiative that Flagstaff was early in instituting. "There are places to improve," she says, "but people care about water issues, about traffic. The city is making a lot of progress on a number of things.

"It's not an apathetic town," says Houk, who looks the part of a quintessential Northern Arizona woman: tanned, serene, comfortable and glowing with life. "You could spend all your time going to public meetings, getting involved in the public process. There are lots of opportunities to participate with local government and get things done."

Houk and her husband, physician and writer Michael Collier, chose Flagstaff as home after their school graduations, and despite frequent travel, still feel no other place would compare.

"I don't want to be too schmaltzy, but it's about the people and the lifestyle," she says. "Even if people leave, a lot of them end up coming back."

Houk loves the combination of people and places that make Flagstaff unique. "For example, we went to dinner at some friends' recently, out in Doney Park. We sat outside, and looked at the cinder hills and pinon and juniper trees. We talked about insects and plant life and forest fires. Then we ended up getting out binoculars looking for birds. There aren't too many places you go to someone's home for dinner and end up doing all that. We might be sitting listening to jazz downtown, or talking environmental issues. It's the scope of life here."

She jokes that in her work writing for magazines, "I never have to make an appointment to see anyone. I just go downstairs and stand on the corner, and sooner or later, everyone walks by." Looking out on Heritage Square, the brick paving glistening from afternoon rain, Houk has high praise for business leaders who have brought free movies to residents during the summer, showing them on a huge white sheet hung against the Babbitt building. She also cites the Painted Sky Music Festival and programs from the university as examples of people creating a vibrant and vital culture. "Every time we take the pulse of Flagstaff and ask ourselves if it's still the place we want to live, we always decide it is."

Good people want the best for Flagstaff. The tough part is agreeing on what that is.

Rob and Elise Wilson love their home near the country club – a back-yard fountain and stream where deer come to drink, room for the two family dogs to play and bark at the thunderstorms. But even more, they love the land.

"The only hard part is watching the trees on it die," says Elise, an energetic woman with shiny hair and an open face. "We keep count how many have been killed by the drought and bark beetles. So we love the rain!"

She says the couple sports "FLG" stickers on their mountain bikes to avoid being taken as tourists. Not that there's anything wrong with them, she hastens to add. It's just that "I love it that it's we who get to live here," she says.

Kurt Davis believes Flagstaff's future hinges on learning to bring in business.

"Flagstaff is truly a beautiful place, filled with pioneering spirit and passionate people; it is also the intersection of several cultures, and has the benefit of a first class university as its heartbeat. However, like any healthy person, along with a good heart there also has to be a strong backbone. In the case of Flagstaff, the backbone has to be a knowledgeable and vibrant econ-omy-based business community that can tap into the intellectual capital pro-duced by NAU. On that count, Flagstaff has a serious risk of 'back problems,' that is, a divisive political and social agenda that can drive away economic opportunity and the middle class with it. That said, the magic of the Flagstaff lifestyle still exists." And to the residents, the magic of the Peaks make the val-leys worthwhile.

ROSE HAUK

ANN FITZPATRICK

PASCUAL RAMIREZ OF CASA GRANDE

CHAPTER 14

CASA GRANDE:
A HOME BIG ENOUGH FOR ALL

Casa Grande may be named after the ruins called "Big House," but it is definitely a small town.

If any community in Arizona embodies contradictions, it is Casa Grande. Named for the Anasazi ruins some miles away, which gives it ancient roots, it is not ancient at all. It is, in fact, awash in new construction. Since it began people have come primarily for jobs – hard work in farming and railroading. Today it is also a mecca for retirees. Casa Grande seems like a place in which not many would choose to live; yet everyone seems unusually proud to call it home. A small, almost Mayberry-type community, it is also one of the most diverse in Arizona, both racially and economically. To outsiders, Casa Grande is a bit of an enigma. To residents, it all makes perfect sense.

Celebrating 125 years in 2004, Casa Grande's ironic beginnings lay in being a surplus yard for railroad construction materials. In 1879, a fed-up Southern Pacific crew walked off the job complaining that the heat was too much to bear. Along with the leftover supplies that were dumped off, a Southern Pacific post office car that had been moving up and down the railroad line was left behind. A new settlement began and was appropriately named "Terminus." Records don't show what enterprising citizen later decided the town might draw more people renamed for the Casa Grande ruins 20 miles away.

It is representative of today's Casa Grande that the story of Terminus is included in the literature at the Visitor's Center downtown. Casa Grande appears completely without pretension, and is as refreshing as a woman in Beverly Hills who lets her hair go gray. Casa Grande does not put on airs. People here are happy with their town the way it is.

The way it is very much comes from being a family town. Self-reliant people who treasure the importance of families, they believe hard work and helping others is a lovely way of life. Regardless of their ethnic and professional differences, they come across as honest and not self-involved people. Of course it's a little hard to come off as pretentious if your shoes still wear the soil of the morning's chores, and the brim of your hat is still moist from a hot afternoon in the Southwestern sun. The life of the town may be changing, but the life of the townsfolk has changed very little.

Casa Grande used to get a lot of passing-through traffic. Traveling from Tucson, whether to California or Northern Arizona, took you up Highway 84, past the incongruously named Snow Flake Inn on Casa Grande's main drive. But when Interstate 10 began streaming with traffic about ten miles east of the town in the 60's, Casa Grande became only an exit sign to many travelers, except those who went west into town on purpose. The construction of outlet stores near the Casa Grande exit in the 80's has given the town a higher profile that residents seem to find amusing.

Bob Mitchell, retired mayor, said that for years when asked where he lived, "Casa Grande" would be met with blank stares. "Now you say 'Casa Grande' and you get, 'Oh, by the outlet mall!' as if that's why we live there. I ask, 'Have you been to Casa Grande?' Usually they haven't."

He is aware that this town he loves is still a hard sell to many. "The Chamber of Commerce wants tourism and the money it can bring," he tells us.

"But people come for the weather, which is hard to show. You can't seem to sell the ruins, and we don't have landmarks. I've thought about our situation a lot."

When Mitchell moved to Casa Grande he had only about 8,000 neighbors. In the 30-plus years since then it's grown to more than 30,000. After college, Mitchell got a teaching position here, and met a lot of the residents. "When you see parents in a store, you can talk. To hear, 'Mom, I want you to meet Mr. Mitchell' is a warm feeling." But even after three decades, Mitchell doesn't see himself as an old-timer. "People are friendly; you're very welcome, but you're always aware of who started here and who didn't. They do always know you're an outsider. People still tell me how things used to be." Then, looking back, there are the stories of farmers who couldn't resist the escalating values of land, particularly if it bordered the freeway, and sold it – for another housing development and thousands of homes.

One member of the old families is Mitchell's friend, Ray Hernandez, a jovial man who remembers all the longtime families, listed as pioneers: Levaria, Echevierra, Salazar and Serrano. Hernandez's grandfather came from Mexico, and his father worked shearing sheep to put his children through school. "Neither parent spoke English," Hernandez says. "I came from the south side of the tracks. We learned to plow and irrigate fields. We also learned to go to school and speak the language." He and eight brothers and sisters became part of the American dream, sending their children on to college. Hernandez himself retired as a general manager for the Southern Pacific, starting in Casa Grande and working his way up to traveling 17 states. When he retired, he never considered living anywhere else. "It's nice to walk down the street and always talk to someone," he shares. "People are willing to get involved. In Casa Grande we go out of our way to build relationships."

Maybe the feeling of Old Casa Grande is preserved because most of the new construction is filling in stretches of desert between the town and the freeway. Driving into town, swoops and curves of stucco walls come one after the other, with framing and bright signs inviting home shoppers to visit the models. These are planned developments, as opposed to the seemingly random construction in the traditional town center. Humble homes, businesses, public buildings and broad ranch houses all share streets in patchwork harmony. On a weekday morning, Casa Grande is quiet, even downtown is not bustling. But there is none of the elegiac, fading quality that some of Arizona's smaller towns evoke. Casa Grande could easily have become a casualty of indifference and a diminishing agricultural economy. People loved it enough to persist in creating new economics.

While not quite the dominant industry of old, the farmers, particularly the cotton growers, are a hardy bunch. Some have responded to the sinking prices by transitioning to soybeans and other crops, but many cotton growers stick it out through the roller coaster of low prices and uncertain water supplies. It's a tough life, for a tough bunch. Many, like the prominent Dugan family, have invested in dairy farms and made a go of it. But whatever pessimism many in agriculture feel, all share an optimism about the future of Casa Grande.

Although the main streets aren't crowded, there is a sense of relevance to them. New ventures flourish. One is the Dorothy Powell Senior Adult Center, a broad, welcoming building. In a bright room filled with chat and laughter, RV'ers and winter visitors share tables. Whether newcomers or visitors, they feel the same sense of belonging that old-time residents describe.

"We like Casa Grande real well," said Phyllis Plotnick, a fulltime RVer who used to live in Hemet, California. She looks up from her card game with three other players. "We came through a couple of times before we retired. We've been all over the country, but you never see sunsets as beautiful as here. The colors in the evenings against the clouds, and the shadows on the mountains...changing as the sun goes down." There is a general murmur of assent from around the card table.

Wanda Johns, another player, nods. After a half-century here, she still remembers her first sunsets. "I would see pictures of them and think, 'Someone colored in that pink, it couldn't be real.' But once I got here...I saw it."

She loves Casa Grande. "This town just gives and gives. We have so many volunteers. When we needed a center for abused children, Sears gave appliances, we had a contractor give his time and expertise; Arizona Public Service gave us land." Prominent attorney David "Red" Fitzgibbons, a lawyer in Casa Grande, learned that the new hospital couldn't afford the latest cardiac scanner, so he started a hospital foundation and raised the money to buy it.

Kathleen Schiefelbein works at the Dorothy Powell Senior Adult Center's front desk. Brochures list the lunch menu for the month, with a reminder that while lunch is two dollars per person, non-members and guests under 60 cost twice that much. Another announcement asks users of van service to make arrangements the previous day, adding that while a trip costs five dollars to provide, only a one-dollar donation is requested. A gift shop sells donated items, as well as t-shirts and cups with the Dorothy Powell Center logo on them. A stamp collector's club is being formed and welcomes new members. With free dance lessons, bingo and support groups, many people have reasons to be here.

Of course, the discounts and services mean donations and volunteers are filling the gap between actual cost and what is charged. Scheifelbein says that is one of Casa Grande's greatest strengths. She cites the center's namesake as an example of Casa Grande's stellar volunteers. Pointing to a painting in the dining room, she proudly but sadly quotes Mrs. Powell: "Age may make your skin wrinkle, but to give up enthusiasm makes your soul wrinkle." Mrs. Powell poured her heart and soul into the three-year old Senior Center, literally until she died. "She drove up here, walked in, and said she didn't feel well and died, right there." Shiefelbein recounts.

A visit to Dorothy's home some years ago was akin to a tour of a Casa Grande historical museum. Clippings from the local newspaper, the Dispatch, social pages adorned the walls, from each of the past four decades and spanning a cornucopia of causes. Her love for Casa Grande was infectious, friends say, and at the Center, her legacy still lives.

Volunteers have carried on her work, serving breakfast to about 100 visitors the first Saturday of each month, making the table decorations, leading sing-alongs on Friday evenings, and setting up coffee and rolls every

Tuesday morning. With computer classes, card games, ceramics and other crafts, Casa Grande seniors make this a home away from home.

Seniors have different ways of keeping busy. On the serene lawns of St. Anthony's Catholic Church, Pascual Ramirez is tending roses and clipping trees just as he did all the years it was his paying job. It's a peaceful place, embodying the sentimental image of the church in an old hometown. A tower rises above the low building; birds seem to congregate in the branches over the smooth lawn. There is an almost palpable serenity, just as inside the scent of candle smoke seems to hold in prayers. The church is the lynchpin of Ramirez's life and has been for years.

"I like to do this, in my heart," he says, leaning on his rake. "My wife used to help me. Father Steve paid me for a long time, then in the 80's he quit, and I said, 'It's okay.' I say they pay me when I die. I hope," he adds, with a small smile that fans wrinkles across a face like tanned leather. When asked it he could be photographed, Ramirez soon digs out a bulging wallet, and intently rifles through looking for something. He finally produces two items. One is a photograph of his knee joint replacement. The reverence with which he points out the replacement parts shows that this technology amazes him. The other item he displays is his church membership card. His identity is tied to giving to this place. He believes that to capture his image, these must be included.

It is this identity with his church that embodies what makes Casa Grande a successful community. "All my kids come here, bring flowers," he says. Pointing at the statue behind him, he adds, "La Virgen, Guadalupe. I put one like it at my house. I want to put roses here next."

His daughter is also named for La Virgen de Guadalupe, he says, and adds proudly that she works nearby. Sure enough, while her father rakes grass clippings to the sound of birdsong, Lupe is getting ready to spend the day serving Mexican food at the Little Sombrero, a pickup restaurant a few blocks away. Asking for directions in Spanish at a corner store gets you from one to the other. Lupe, a pretty, practical-looking woman with her hair bound back, agrees to take a moment to visit only when urged by her co-workers. Not a woman looking for a spotlight, she opens up when told her father spoke of her.

"I live here because I was born here," she says. "All my kids were born here too. I think it's okay."

She has worked at Little Sombrero for 25 years, since she graduated from high school. Her children now also attend the same church as their grandfather. It wasn't until two years ago that she needed a driver's license to get her children to all their activities. "The town's growing," she reflects. "But it's okay. People here are all nice. We get a lot of regulars."

Most people seem to be regulars in Casa Grande. Some gather at the Little Sombrero. Some habituate The Property, while Dispatch Publisher Donovan Kramer and son frequent The Cookie Jar. But everyone has a routine. It is the Mayberry way to stay in trade.

Maybe it's normal in Casa Grande to be able to walk a few blocks to see your father or daughter. But in a state where the average resident moves every three years, and most neighbors can't name five families on their street, this sense of roots and permanence seems a beautiful thing to behold.

Casa Grande isn't just dependent on small businesses. The economy now has corporate and chain commerce, such as the Francisco Grande Resort and Golf Club, a gracious sprawl of white stucco and breezeways inviting leisurely pursuits. Wal-Mart is here, Frito-Lay and the Casa Grande Regional Medical Center. Quite a contrast to the old days of farms and railroads.

"I loaded boxcars," says Mitchell of his teenage years. "I got 87 cents an hour to put boxes of onions on cars in Higley. The Spanish workers got 75 cents, but also room and board."

"There was a bracero program in the 50's," recalls Hernandez. "I worked in Stanfield in a fabric store. We were open till midnight on weekends. It didn't make much sense till I found out we sold mostly money orders, and the workers would come in to send money home to Mexico."

Dolly Echeverria married into one of the old sheep ranching families. "Since the sheep were in Picacho, Eloy, Coolidge, Florence, we were like gypsies," she explains. "We would rent the grazing land at so much per day. The fencing wasn't electric then, just wire and steel post."

Echeverria is another of the old names.

"Some people were saying recently that back in high school, you couldn't throw a rock without hitting an 'Ecchie,'" she says. Because she stayed home to raise her children, she drove carloads of girls on camping trips, attended hundreds of sports practice sessions, and was always available in an emergency.

"I remember once a nurse at the hospital telling me, 'You know, there really is a front door. You always come in Emergency,' " she recalls. "They always asked if the child being treated was mine, and sometimes I crossed my fingers before I said 'yes.' "

One of the best aspects of Casa Grande to her is the broad ethnic representation. "We had so many minorities. All the kids were exposed to many different cultures; they absorbed a lot of sophistication for a town this size."

Another resident who glories in the diversity is retired basketball coach Al Van Hazel. Coming to Casa Grande in 1948, he had the longest tenure of any teacher in the system, and is a legend, if not an icon, in this town. Few Casa Grande families missed being in his classroom in the past 50 years. Van Hazel coached football, track and basketball, making less than $3,000 the first year. "That included digging the track and watering it, and everything else.

"There was never any trouble, even with all the different kids," he says. "I told them I was the biggest minority in the whole county, because I'm Dutch. I said, 'We're the wetbacks – my dad came across the Atlantic. A lot of your folks just crossed the Rio Grande.'"

Get a few men who grew up in Casa Grande together, and Van Hazel's name invariably comes up. Hernandez is one of his alumni.

"My brothers were here recently, and we all went to visit Van Hazel," he says. "He was the happiest guy I've seen in a long time. He said looking back, every team he'd had for years had either a Hernandez or a Levaris on it." Hernandez remembers playing a nearby town and being told the two black members of the team couldn't stay in the hotel when they went to check in. "So we all moved to another hotel."

Kevin White, now a judge for Pinal County, was one of Van Hazel's players on the Casa Grande Cougars. "When you're all thrown together, you can't help but mix," he proclaims. "We had African Americans, Native Americans, Asians, and Hispanics. We didn't know till later it wasn't that way every place."

White still reaps the benefits of that background. The high school teens who played together have retained the sense of friendly competition.

"Today a fellow Cougar player was in my court," he says. "I actually threatened him with contempt and jail during the proceedings, and at the end he said, 'See you, Kevin,' on the way out." These are the unbreakable bounds of community. It is little surprise that he moved back to Casa Grande after working in both Phoenix and Washington D.C. "I'd say Casa Grande was always the place I envisioned myself. In a big city, you're just an anonymous face in the crowd. I went east, but I knew I would come back. I see now why my parents and brothers chose to stay." He has three children under the age of six, "And they're staying here forever."

There is little question that the place is changing demographically. The forbidding cost of land in Maricopa County has pushed developers south into Pinal County. Casa Grande is now closer to many of the Valley employers, particularly around Chandler, than any other affordable housing in Maricopa County. With the explosive growth – twelve to fifteen new developers -- the community is faced with extraordinary opportunity: a bigger and broader tax base, higher disposable income. But this also brings many challenges, most notably how to preserve the agricultural sector that has been both an economic foundation and a way of life. Water management gets more crucial. Perhaps most importantly for this town of natural familiarity, will the new residents look south to Casa Grande as a community to become immersed in? Or simply stay nestled in their grand cul de sac? When the newbies discover Casa Grande they may love it, and the people who made it.

Unlike other Arizona towns that are known for spectacular scenery or picturesque streets, Casa Grande gets its sense of community from the people. This makes it less of an instant draw compared, to, say, Prescott and its Victorian homes, or Sedona and its red rocks. But it also offers protection from those who would live in such places for status or external beauty.

For the people who love the area, the important things remain. Viva Mitchell moved here from nearby Arizona City eleven years ago. She remembers when "it was just a little town surrounded by cotton fields." "It's grown quite a bit, but it's still good. It's quiet, and not congested. And it cools down at night."

Casa Grande is "Big House" and the town of Casa Grande is big houses and big families, where all are welcome to come and stay. Casa Grande may be named for an ancient ruin, but it also aptly describes a special community, with big hearts and a big welcome for anyone who wants to feel the same way.

JUDGE KEVIN WHITE

CASA GRANDE SENIOR CENTER

PATAGONIA LAKE

CHAPTER 15

BORDERLANDS:
BETWEEN TWO WORLDS

O nly a century and a half ago, there was no Arizona. All the land now included in the 48th state belonged to Mexico. Now an imaginary line, stitched by fences, a ditch, and a couple of crossing points, signifies the border between two nations, and two worlds.

To tourists traveling south to Nogales, crossing the border may be a nuisance, or a sobering reminder that you are not in Arizona any more. Just beyond the guards, the gates, the monitoring stations, you already have a look at life so near, yet so far from your own. An aggressive, slightly built boy wants to sell you chewing gum, whether you want to buy it or not. A woman who is probably younger than she looks sits on the curb, with her two children playing in the stream of brown water flowing past her feet. The older child wears faded blue pajamas with feet, pilled and stained. The smaller child is crawling in the muddy water in a diaper. The mother stares straight ahead, paying no attention. A little farther down the street, a man with a docile donkey will take your photo with an instant camera. You can wear the sombrero if you want. There are leather stores, liquor stores, perfume and pottery shops. You have to drive awhile to get to the green, rolling, rural Mexico. Beyond are the beaches, villas, and soldiers. But here, on this street, you see almost a caricature of border life.

On the Arizona side, north of the actual dividing line, the border is an area, not a gate. It is a nether zone, part of Arizona, but it is far more immersed in what lies to the south than most people imagine.

PATAGONIA

Driving south toward Patagonia, you have to know how many tenths of a mile to go past a marker to turn in, or miss the Amado family ranch completely. It looks like something from an old Western movie. The arched gate bearing the Amado brand framing pastoral sweeps of grass, under wide gentle skies. Horses graze, breezes rustle – all it lacks is background music. When Henry Amado rides his land he is doing what his father and grandfather and great-grandfather did before him. Amados have been here since long before statehood.

Henry Amado has fragile documents from his ancestors on his father's side, who came from Spain in the 1840's. His mother's relatives sailed from Spain to Mexico in 1711; the Gastelums were Basque, and emigrated to what is now Tubac. "When the Gadsden Purchase was signed in 1853, everyone who was born north of the line became naturalized Americans," says Amado. Families of prosperous ranchers and merchants belonged "…pretty much to a class system," he says. "They would only marry other Spaniards." The Amados ran cattle from Nogales to Cortaro. Henry's great-grandfather, Santos Amado, had a dairy at San Xavier. He also sold grain and supplies to the troops at Fort Lowell.

"At our ranch, we do things pretty much the way they have always been done. We do have a calf table – it's better than branding off a horse. But the brand is the same one my great-grandfather had."

Amado handles the long iron rod with "MA" with reverence. He runs his cattle on 25,000 acres near Patagonia. "We aren't the kind who want to retire," he says of himself and his wife, Laurie. "This is our legacy, and our heritage."

"It's not just what we do," Laurie agrees. "It's a way of life."

It is Laurie's eye for design and décor that make the old caretaker's house a rustic showplace. She can sketch out with a graceful gesture where the next home and guest quarters will be, how the patio will connect. Her success with the Kaibab shops in Tucson is a source of pride to her husband. Laurie would rather speak of her volunteer work and their children. Good naturedly, she supervises the help preparing for roundup that weekend.

"We use a limited number of hired cowboys," Henry says. "The neighboring ranchers come to help, and we, in turn, help them. Everybody's happy to do it. You can't find the same kind of sincerity and honesty in ranchers in other places. You call if you find a cow that's wandered to your property. You could call a livestock inspector, but it's more neighborly to just take it over. Since the early days, a rancher's word has been gold."

While Laurie will supervise barbecues and huge breakfasts to feed the working neighbors in the tradition of many decades, some things have changed since the early days. "Now, the cowboys are afraid to leave their females alone on their ranches," says Amado. "In the old days, if you left home you would leave the ranch house open. If someone needed to eat, they were welcome to help themselves. These days they're going to break in and steal from you."

The undocumented Mexicans coming up across the ranchlands of southern Arizona are a problem. "We worry they're drug smugglers," says Laurie.

"I see them when I'm out alone on horseback," adds Henry. "Last time there were fifteen or twenty guys laying in a hollow by a stream that always runs. I went over and said, 'Resting? Well, get along now.'"

He would rather be like his mother, he says. "She welcomed illegals. When we were kids, they came, did whatever jobs needed doing around the ranch, stayed a day or two and then they were gone. Nowadays everyone is afraid to help them. It's against the law. If you pick up an illegal, you've got a problem."

In the big picture, however, the Amados don't consider this to be a big problem for them. Anyway, the ranching life is the only one they want.

"I don't know if it's my imagination," says Henry, "but when I leave Tucson on Friday afternoon and get to the Thurber Ranch, it feels like I'm entering a different world."

"As soon as you come through the gate, your blood pressure drops," adds Laurie. She describes parties with a hundred guests, mariachis, tables of steaks, green corn tamales and beans.

"It's about memories," says Henry. "When I get together with my brothers and my cousins, we reminisce about life on the ranch. What's important to us is that the kids remember things here, like the first time they went on a roundup."

Sonoita

The Amados have the ranching life in their blood and bones. Other people followed them later. Just north of Patagonia, Sonoita is growing as newcomers discover the open sky and gentle hills of the area. Mild in climate and gaining fame as wine country, Sonoita is waiting in the wings to become as sought after as places like Sedona and Angel Fire. Retired moguls and magnates wander down to the crossroads that define the town, drift into shops to browse, have lunch at unassuming cafes, and catch up on the local news. An eclectic mix of artists, philanthropists and horse enthusiasts have ranches and casitas in the spreading grassland beyond.

Sinclair Browning is an author and Arizonan. She and her husband Bill, known to most in the state as retired Federal Judge William Browning, have lived in the grassy southlands of the state for five years. They sit on their patio on a breezy day, sipping coffee while hummingbirds ricochet around the edges of the roof darting from one feeder to the next. Down the slope their horses graze in a neat corral. The rammed-earth house, full of charm and rustic furnishings, evokes a ranch house from a century before. But it has a burglar alarm, mostly because of the passing traffic of undocumented workers. The rutted road with a cattle guard they cross in their huge four-wheel drive pickup is crossed by a large electronic gate. Even in Sonoita, you can find a gated community now.

"It's the sort of elitism I've hated all my life," says Bill. "Now, I love it." Bill Browning's looks could be right off a ranching spread from another era: white hair brighter over his tanned face, slightly stooped but clearly strong enough to handle hay or horses. He touches his wife on the shoulder when he passes her, just because. Sinclair draws her listener in with an all-embracing gaze and animated countenance. Both in denim, they seem organic to their surroundings.

While she loves the acreage and quiet of their ranch, Sinclair says it now comes at a price: Illegals coming up from Mexico. "We are totally impacted by border issues," she says. "Even when we lived in Tucson, we had no clue how bad it is down here.

"A couple of weeks ago, an illegal walked up the road here and begged us for money," Sinclair reports. "The manager of the Rail X Ranch says dozens come through there every night. At the Rose Tree, three illegals froze to death. It's a big problem. I don't want them to starve to death, but I don't want them here. I don't think of myself as a racist in any way; I grew up in Tanque Verde Ranch playing with all the Mexican children. But if I wanted to live in Mexico, I'd live there. That's why I turn in every one I see."

Sinclair is frustrated with the federal system on the border.

"It's a federal mandate that you have to close all the border stations during rain," she continues. "It's too dangerous chasing anyone on slick roads. So as soon as it rains, the border stations close, and there are men on cell phones calling for vans that go shooting up the highway."

Another problem that began as a solution was the policy of returning undocumented workers to their homes in interior Mexico, rather than just dropping them on the other side of the border. While the thinking was that it would take them longer to return that way, Sinclair points out that this is also a "taxi service" for the drug dealers and "coyotes," who can, then, immediately return, bringing another profitable load of narcotics or people north. "You see them everyday, healthy young men walking slowly up the road, looking over their shoulders for the Border Patrol to come pick them up and take them back home."

"Coyotes charge $1500 to bring an illegal across," she says. "But that includes three tries. This is for Mexicans. The 'hot' countries, the Middle Eastern countries, it costs more. Those are OTMs – Other Than Mexicans. And now the Border Patrol says a third of those who cross have felony charges against them. Sometimes they sacrifice a big load of drugs to get more people across."

"By and large, most of these people are not criminals," Bill interjects. "Even though they could steal, they mostly don't. But our cows die, eating their trash. One rancher cuts the bottom half of his barbed wire fence out, for them to come under, because otherwise they cut through it and the cows get out. Sometimes they've broken in and stolen coats. Once they ate a rancher's ice cream. Another time they took whiskey in a wheelbarrow, and all the guy's low-carb tortillas; that was like a stake in his heart, having to replace the tortillas."

"They know there's a better life here, and they want to feed their families," he says. "If I were down there, I'd be trying the same thing."

Sonoita is clearly ranch country; further east along the border life is less about cattle and more about industry.

DOUGLAS

Douglas began as a mining town. A century ago, residents said the prettiest sight to see in Douglas was the smoke belching from the twin smokestacks of the copper smelter Phelps Dodge built to help process Bisbee ore. Those smokestacks were shut down in 1987 after years of wrangling with the Environmental Protection Agency. Today, Douglas may be proudest of the

Gadsden Hotel, approaching its centennial, and one of the last great old hotels in Arizona. Marble pillars, gold leaf detailing, and striking mission-style stained glass make the lobby a place out of time. It is a monument to survival and resilience. Douglas evokes the feeling of a small midwestern town, with houses lining wide streets, a quaint downtown, and an unusual plethora of parks. Just beyond the businesses and boundaries lies nothing but barren desert.

Talking to Douglas residents, one gets a sense of fortitude equal to their forbearers. A town completely shaped by mining and proximity to the border, it has none of Sonoita's Big Sky cinema ease. Here, hard work and tradition are steeped in every house. These are people who acknowledge the past without bitterness, which can be hard to do just hearing their stories.

"We had an enormous amount of pollution," says Mike Garino. "If the wind blew south into Mexico, Phelps Dodge opened all the valves. You couldn't see five feet in front of you. PD said, 'That isn't pollution, that's progress.' But the sulfur ate through television cables that were supposed to last 15 years in a third of that time." Mike adds that when PD shut down, the town still had the "owe my soul to the company store" mentality. "It took a while to get over it."

Mike and his wife Olivia Garino both grew up here. In fact, Olivia was in first grade when she decided the second grade boy who would become her husband, was her boyfriend, even before knowing his name. A retired teacher, Mike taught several generations before moving to Cochise College. Olivia teaches folklorico to high school students, dances she began learning at age five. Their home was once a guest house for Phelps Dodge managers, which they find ironic because back then, "anyone whose name ended in 'o' didn't even visit, let alone live there."

Joaquin Livia smiles, hearing this. He also grew up south of the smelters in the informally but rigidly segregated town. As a child, he suffered from the smelter emissions with asthma so severe he slept sitting up. "You could even feel it get into your mouth," he says. Still, his parents joined virtually everyone in town in a conspiracy of silence in order to keep the smelters in operation.

"Pressure was put on to do it," says Livia. "Studies showed that emissions from Douglas showed up as far away as Phoenix. But PD kept stalling, saying that to put in scrubbers would bankrupt the company. PD threatened to leave. A big hearing was held in the early 80's for state officials to learn 'the facts' from local people. Everyone told them there was no health hazard. PD was the life of the community, and everyone rallied around it. So the community gave PD a few more years by lying about their health just to keep them here."

Ramon and Lupe Jordan have seen it all here in Douglas, and most of it together. Married for 61 years, Ramon says he didn't know until they applied for a marriage license that his bride had been 12 when they met at a softball field. Lupe contends she didn't know the real name of the boy they always called "Hedgie" till she saw the license.

Ramon says his father came from Mexico in 1912, when El Paso opened the border because workers were needed in town. "As they came across, they were sprayed with disinfectant," he says. None of the children were born until his parents were in the United States. "Thank God," he says. Ramon recounts that in his childhood, many friends accepted a financial bonus for returning to Mexico, but his family stayed. There was work in the mines, although the pay scale was higher for Anglos than for Hispanics.

Both Lupe and Ramon remember when Anglo and Hispanic students went to segregated schools, and even at their own school students who spoke Spanish on the playground were punished. "There was a lot of discrimination when we were growing up," says Lupe. "We couldn't go to dances at our own high school."

They may have all been United States citizens, but at PD, Ramon was never allowed to forget his father was from Mexico. He tells of going into the company stores speaking Spanish and being unable to get anyone to wait on him. After a shift at the smelter, he and his friends had to shower at different times from the Anglos. Later, says Ramon, "Phelps Dodge paid higher wages to us only when they had to, when even Anglos wouldn't work those jobs."

Maybe it is partly because many Douglas residents are descended from Mexico that the sister city, Agua Prieta, enjoys essentially equal status. More lyric than the English translation, "muddy water," and usually referred to as "AP," traffic flows both ways across the border. Ginny Jordan, who helps small businesses get funding in the area, says medical care is much cheaper south of the border.

"Both my daughters got their braces for their teeth in AP," she says. "A lot of us go across for dental and eye care. You can even get plastic surgery across the line." She says the crossing is generally quick and easy. "They also have a mall and a Cineplex, and more hotels than we have here."

But Agua Prieta residents come up to Douglas to shop at Wal-Mart, and to use the library. Glinda Bavier, a librarian here, says she issues cards to residents of both towns. "It's really one community," she says. "I hear forty percent of our sales tax revenue here is from the south. And for every two dollars we spend there, one comes back.

"People drop their laundry in AP. It's cheaper, and they probably do a better job. I love to go to dinner there. Since I don't speak Spanish, to me it's like visiting another culture – like going to Europe, only it's a few blocks away."

Residents are concerned that as feelings run higher against illegal immigration, conditions may become less flexible. Since most Douglas residents have relatives living south of the border, they feel part of one community, not separate nations. Ironically, the Border Patrol has replaced the mines as the main source of jobs. "If the Border Patrol left, you would see property values plummet," says one resident.

So while family members utilize the border as a porous web of services, they also want the controls set up to prevent illegal crossing to flourish. A contradiction indeed, but one that can be accepted – one that makes sense to those living in Douglas.

Life along the border has always been difficult from the time the arbitrary boundaries created by the Gadsden Purchase changed the citizenship of residents literally overnight. From the days of land grants made by Spaniards of territory that was Indian land, technicalities have butted heads with daily life. The law and living have learned to co-exist. In some ways, this defines the two worlds of the borderlands more than the national boundaries ever will.

As border problems gain more national attention, people in the ranchlands and towns deal with the issues as they always have: with both acceptance and frustration. But no one talks about moving. This is home, an Arizona with wilder roots and maybe more determined ancestors. They know things will not be black and white in this country.

BROWNINGS

HENRY AMADO

Sonoita Barn

SUN CITY GOLFERS

CHAPTER 16

SUN CITIES:
NEW PIONEERS

HOW PIONEERS HAVE CHANGED!

One of the first Anglos to settle in the valley northwest of Phoenix was Henry Wickenberg, who was throwing rocks at his donkey to move him in whatever direction Wickenberg thought fate should direct him to make a mining claim. The stubborn donkey didn't help in the decision, but the third rock Wickenberg picked up was heavy with gold. The town was named for him the next year.

A century later, a new breed of pioneer was settling the northwest valley; people who had pulled up roots and came searching for a different kind of gold. These were the early residents of Sun City, coming to make their golden years shine. The first generation of Sun City residents were like the first class of a new high school: an inaugural collective of people embarking on an untried adventure, sharing the sensations of this big clean slate, completely open and inviting, while also completely empty of memory and devoid of a support system.

These first residents experienced versions of the trials and the freedom of those earlier Arizonans who came from other places and built new lives. They were drawn together to make decisions about their new town, and forged bonds that were made stronger by their common condition. Those who moved to Sun City between 1960 and 1975 share the memories of Les Parry, who was in charge of quality control, meeting them at their new front door, presenting them with a key, and walking through the home with them, explaining, asking, suggesting. Those first residents created the first 100 clubs in Sun City. More than 15,000 of them were the planning committee, of sorts, for their common home.

While Sun Cities and Del Webb are linked in social consciousness as introducing retirement communities and leisure living, they both began elsewhere.

In the 1940's, enjoying retirement became a part of the public aware-ness. A newspaper ad selling insurance used the line, "The joy of being at the ballpark on a weekday afternoon." In 1954, an article in Business Week pointed out, "Most workers are pathetically unprepared for retirement. They are financially secure but are faced with large blocks of time and nothing to fill the empty hours." But even with that realization, architect and urban his-torian Lewis Mumford wrote disparagingly about the concept of retirement communities. "The worst possible attitude toward old age is to regard the aged as a segregated group...to live in desolate idleness, relieved only by others in a similar plight." (Interestingly, in an early Congressional report of the land that now contains Sun Cities stated, "This region is altogether worthless. After entering it, there is really nothing to do but leave.")

As the father of Sun Cities, no one could have been more of a boot-strap pioneer than Del Webb. Born in 1899 in Fresno, Webb tagged along watching his father do construction work during his childhood. Webb worked in shipyards during World War I, and followed his father into the construction business. One job he held was as a door-hanger for the Westward Ho in down-town Phoenix in 1927. When another contractor defaulted on the job, Webb took over his work, and began his career as a contractor with the ten wheelbarrows, twenty shovels and ten picks abandoned by the defunct firm.

Although he later wrote that he tried to get out of building the Las Vegas Flamingo when he found out Bugsy Seigel, who was "intimately connected with the mafia," was the money behind it, Webb moved into other notable construction projects, including the Beverly Hills Hilton, the United States Pavilion for the New York World's Fair, and the Mountain Shadows Resort in Scottsdale.

Webb's first planned communities were far different than his later golden-age metropolises. The government contract work that made him his first real money during World War II included creating the Japanese Relocation Camp near Parker, Arizona. From there he moved on to construct-ing more diverse communities that included parks and stores, among which was San Manuel for the Phelps Dodge Copper Company. In 1957 when some of his employees saw an NBC piece about Youngtown, a new retirement community northwest of Phoenix, Webb resisted the idea of entering the retirement market. With only twenty percent of homebuyers falling into the retirement age group, he was reluctant to embark on such a venture.

When more than 100,000 people flocked to the first three days of the Grand Opening, Webb realized that this was indeed a gold mine of another type and he planned his first retirement community, Sun City. In a master stroke of marketing, everyone who bought in Sun City was asked to answer questions about what was important in a new home and new community. The feedback from residents helped him shape the sister communities that would follow. Del Webb opened Sun City in 1960, and the market responded so enthusiastically that he began planning Sun City West before the Sun City models were all sold. Sun City Grand is the most recent, and like many youngest children, the most indulged. Homes are noticeably higher end, with bigger lots and more luxury features.

After 45 years, Sun City is starting to show its age: the streets and homes have a uniformity that have become passé. Cream, beige, ivory, the houses lay out in curving rows like cards from a deck, orderly but anonymous. Sun City West appears to have made a conscious effort to permit owners to imprint a bit of their own style. And Sun City Grand homes, which can cost ten times as much as a Sun City resale, echo the buyer-decides mindset of the 21st century: customize, customize, customize – as long as everything is in keeping with CC&Rs (Covenants, Conditions and Regulations) rigorous enough to keep property values up.

One thing the Sun Cities have in common is utter cleanliness. "You drive in and it's just perfect," says Bonnie Boyce-Wilson, a Sun City West resident. "The common areas are just pristine. There's not a piece of paper lying anywhere. And that is all volunteer effort."

There is a tranquility that is almost a studied ease, with benches strategically placed near fountains, and restaurants with floral curtains and plantation decor. In some places, above the carefully neutral houses accented by palm trees, the sky looks empty instead of expansive. Diversity may be a goal, but the population in the last census was still 99 percent Caucasian. This is not a noisy, sprawling, colorful place. In fact, its appeal lies in the opposite direction: people have done extensive research to find a home that offers what they want to count on: sunshine, like-minded neighbors, and lots to do. "We did a lot of searching for five or six years," says Boyce-Wilson. "We took our time. We think the homes have character, and they include all the activities. Sun City West has more than a hundred charter clubs. If you can't find something to do, you're just lazy or not trying." This sentiment is echoed frequently among residents.

Lola Boan loves the area. "I can walk anywhere, and feel very safe," she says. "As a single woman, I can do a lot of things I couldn't do other places. I can go to the theater, golf, exercise, travel."

Boan isn't exaggerating. At the SCW Recreation Center office brochures compete for counter space, touting the options for residents with time to fill. More than a dozen excursions on one month's list include everything from a day trip to the zoo to tours with deluxe accommodations in Southern California. Cruises, theater, sightseeing trips mean being with people in your own age group and common interests – a far cry from someone in Boise deciding to set off on a Greyhound.

The clubs are another way to find your own kind of friends. The Sun City Recreation Center, a complex so shiny it looks brand new, shares a parking lot with the SunDome. Inside, residents are getting to indulge in hobbies and past-times that were put on hold until retirement.

In the Railroad Club room, trains wind through scenery as elaborate and interesting as some full-size railroad routes. Some of the men seem to be enjoying the camaraderie even more than the mechanics. Women in the sewing room may be making "Cozy Caps" for cancer patients. Whether one's specialty is cutting, straight seams or ideas, everyone is united in the project. While Sun City West is about as opposite from a small mid-western town as it could be, the feeling in this room is that of a quilting bee in a family home, where everyone gathers to talk, work, and help.

The lapidary shop leans toward more solitary activity while Bowling, billiards and bocce ball call the more social members. Inside a rec center you see the best of Sun Cities: healthy active adults enjoying their free time with friends. But out on the streets, it's hard not to notice how many clinics and health care centers crop up in Sun City. The down side of retirement communities lies in seeing the ill health and frailty that are inevitable. Drive a little farther, however, and wait for golf carts to cross in front of you filled with short-haired women laughing in the sun, whose bright white shorts set off strong tanned legs.

Each Sun City community goes through the growing pains of various life stages in order. Sun City entered the aging crisis first. With an average age of 80, the original buyers' homes are now resales, or inherited by offspring who keep them as winter homes or rent them out. This creates a different type of community. "It affects activities," says Boyce Wilson. "There are fewer rounds of golf as the age of people increases. There's been lots of community controversy over what to do if the golf course use falls too low. Go public is one option; increase fees is another. People fight both of those. No one's closed a course yet, but it may be an option."

What Sun City faces today, the other two communities watch closely. Sun City West averages a population about ten years behind, with Sun City Grand another decade removed. So the quarter-million dollar homebuyers there don't feel the first wave passing unless they seek it out. But Sun City West residents are keenly conscious that their future is playing itself out across Bell Road.

One of the most intriguing aspects of Sun Cities is the future. Michael Whiting, general manager of the Sun City West Recreation Center, is only too aware that in just five years (2000-2005) more than six billion retirees have swollen the potential market for retirement communities.

"I think our future depends on our ability to find what the new demographics will demand," he says. "That will be an exercise in studying, trying to figure out what the baby boomers want, and how we will fit in. We obviously can't compete with some developments because they will have everything new and we will have to retrofit to meet the needs. We have plans to do that. Every year, you have to keep at it. You don't do one study and have all the answers. There will be some surprises, but we'll do our best to really figure it out."

Walking outside, seeing the silver-haired men on the shuffleboard courts, brings to mind men in their 50's still in the work force. Men who marched against the Vietnam War and still set out to hike mountains for fun; men who would rather see Santana than a big band concert. How will Sun Cities cater to people who eschew retirement images of velour jogging suits and card games in favor of khaki and wilderness experiences as sports?

Sun Cities are home to thousands of retirees but even in this age market, this will not be the last home for some. Residents who are passionate about how great the living is here talk freely. It is more difficult to find those who are less delighted. But they are here...and looking to leave. "When I can, I'm going to New Mexico," proclaims one resident of a dozen years. "Everything I came for is ruined. Pollution is terrible, the growth is out of control, and the state legislature – I can't stand those guys!"

Because cheap land is one of Arizona's big draws, growth robs residents of the values that attracted them in the first place: open space and clean air that translate into a broad sense of freedom and the promise of a second chance. Once here, residents are alarmed at governmental policy they may not have investigated before moving.

"I find it offensive how the Arizona Legislature treats education," says Doris Flax, laying to waste the reputation of retirees not caring about schools. She attributes some citizen apathy to the fact that transplants seem to hug their image of "back home" as armor from being assimilated. To her it makes the state a collection of reluctant tenants instead of community builders. There is no metaphorical barn raising: everyone wants to go home, and let someone else solve the problems. "I can't say I'm excited about living in Arizona. And the Arizona Republic's 'News From Home' encourages everyone to think they are still residents of somewhere else. I don't mean to be angry about it. Since education is my focus, it may be my perception is skewed."

Ralph Fischrup detests growth and sprawl filling what was natural desert when he moved here, but says the crisis will come and to some extent resolve itself. "Really, the supply of water determines everything. We'll end up solving some of our problems because if the water isn't there, the population growth can't take place."

"It's greed," says Lola Boan. "Make money, and people don't care about anyone else, or the future." She also thinks people too rooted in their former life don't bring enough to the party. "I feel retired people come here, with the attitude of, 'I retired as an executive.' And they want to keep their status, so they can feel important. They want to have the power. But they don't want to work to earn it." But despite the negatives, she is optimistic about the future. "Young people have a different attitude toward growth. And I think the state will be more open to change compared to ten years ago. We'll care more about air quality, environment and education."

While this is traditionally a liberal view, it is echoed by members of the Rotary Club. Of the 80 or so guests at a meeting, about eight are women, and one hazards a guess that 95 percent are Conservative. The traditions that are easy to lampoon live on: A genial gentleman leading the group in "My Wild Irish

Rose," the joshing and jabbing about being mentioned in the newspaper, the trivia questions to raise funds a dollar at a time. But alongside these benign amusements is pervasive social consciousness: discussion of Rotary participation in a new Pakistan testing lab for the polio-eradication program, signing up for the golf tournament to benefit the Kids' Café of the Westside Food Bank and the West Valley Child Crisis Center. One member talks about the Russian orphan he and his wife adopted – even though the bylaws of Sun City meant they had to relocate to Surprise with the eight-year-old joining the household.

The speech after lunch is about growth, and the buzz of concern over water, environment and spending covers the room. When told 383 people move to Arizona daily, someone calls out, "Too many!"

Suzanne Porter doesn't care for the rapid growth. ("There are hundreds of homes going in around Lake Pleasant; I liked it when it was cotton fields.") She says she might end up in Payson, but Arizona has captured her heart.

Ralph Fischrup agrees the past looks better in soft focus than in reality.

"If it weren't for my health, we'd probably still be in Oregon, which was heaven after Chicago. I was forced out by the weather, but when we went back for two months, that's not somewhere I want to live. I came to peace with it, and let it go. I'm here now."

Sun Cities are as fluid as any Arizona community, but with a special challenge: the burgeoning population of retirement-age residents, not just in Arizona, but nationwide, looking for a better future. Those already here deserve credit for pioneer spirit. Unlike retirees in small towns around the Midwest, none are here by default or inertia. Every one made a conscious choice to move to a new land. Therefore they are not overstaying their welcome at an offspring's home; they are not complaining about where they live but doing nothing about it. They have uprooted their traditions, emptied their garage of things they didn't want to move, saving their children the job of doing it later. They have come to a new place where they aren't known for their position or family name. They have given up a lot, in exchange for more golf days and a readymade peer group. In the spirit of Horace Greeley's encouragement, they have chosen to go west, even though they are young only in spirit. Perhaps that is the most refreshing aspect of Sun Cities: the enthusiastic belief that life can be more or better, or at the very least, warmer, than it has been.

As one genial resident put it, "People here are like the weather: nice every day."

SWIMMING

BILLIARDS

SEDONA CHAPEL

CHAPTER 17

SEDONA:
SEEING THE LIGHT

S edona, in Oak Creek Canyon, sends out its siren song to many. Not surprising, since the red sandstone and blue skies are a constantly changing light show, from the deep auburn panorama of cliffs against cellophane dawn, to the crags of rust, bronze and copper glowing against afternoon skies as deeply turquoise as the finest in a Navajo necklace. With the constant music and murmur of the creek winding through, the green of summer grass and brilliant finale of changing leaves in autumn, this place is a visual feast, pageant, banquet. The only problem might arise if the banquet draws too many guests. Many of those who come and gaze upon the vistas stay. They have seen the light, and they want to bask in it.

Growth in the town of Sedona has accelerated at an increasing rate since its inception in 1902 when Theodore Carl Schnebly applied to be the first postmaster. Bringing his family out from Missouri rounded out the number of homes in the area to an even half-dozen. Told that "Schnebly Station" would take up more of the cancellation circle than "Arizona Territory" left open, T.C. took his brother's suggestion, and named the tiny community after Sedona, his wife.

For reasons lost to the mists of time, Amanda Miller bestowed a poetic name with no known origin on only one of her twelve children. When Sedona and T.C. came west, they brought three-year-old Ellsworth and baby Pearl. Years later Ellsworth wrote about living in tents while the two-story wood house was being built, and finding a plethora of arrowheads as he and Pearl played. The arrowhead opportunities have dwindled to almost nothing, but visitors are still drawn to the ruins and ancient settlements of the Sinagua. Their descendents, the Yavapai Apaches, continue to make pilgrimages to sites in Oak Creek Canyon for ceremonies.

They are not the only ones. Either by buying maps and going out in a four-wheel drive, or signing up for one of the many tours available, people visit not only the ruins, but also monuments that have been added more recently – medicine wheels and cairns of rock created by pilgrims of what's known as New Age thinking. The town of Sedona emerged as a major player leading up to the Harmonic Convergence in August of 1987, a day when some claimed a five-thousand-year cycle of violence ended and peace began. Enthusiasts said the energy of the earth was rapidly increasing, picked up by a quickening of the base frequency of vibrations. Sedona was touted as a place of vortex points where this energy escapes the earth. Stonehenge, Machu Puchu, Oak Creek Canyon and various mountains in Washington State shared top billing as places to experience the full rush of the Harmonic Convergence.

That, in turn, has attracted what is loosely known as the New Age contingent, people who study auras, energies, natural healing and pagan religion (not that these things are necessarily connected). Open a Sedona telephone book and you might notice names that don't remind you of friends from your home town: Ayande One With Creation and Ramona Coyote have both been quoted in media coverage of Sedona. Businesses catering to seekers of energy and chakra wisdom sprang up around town. You can have your aura photographed, select crystals with various healing powers, receive many types of massage, meditation and past life therapy. (Because every reaction has one opposite and equal, there are also occasional flare-ups of blood for sale and various rumors of satanic practices at the medicine wheels and vortexes.) Some mock it, some swear by it, but either way "new age" has become an aspect of Sedona culture.

What makes Sedona different than many Arizona towns is that there are no accidental residents. The cost of land has soared. There are few middle-class jobs. It is an extremely voluntary population. People who have watched the light move across the landscape, changing the colors, had to make it their own. There are people who made a comfortable living and have retired with assets, celebrities in every field who want a refuge. New millionaires who can work anywhere they can plug in a modem gravitate to Sedona.

Joella Jean Mahoney is a charismatic woman with flowing white hair. Her jewelry and manner are arresting and elegant. An artist, she saw the light and wanted to capture it forever on canvas for others. She believes what draws people here and makes them feel more alive are the colors.

"Beauty is seductive," she says. "We are told all these mystical reasons for why we live here, but it's because color pulls up feelings. When we come, we get in touch with lots of personal feelings. We get divorced, we start new relationships. It's all beauty, awe and wonder, that makes us appreciate being alive, and gives us vitality."

She feels that New Age enterprise has cheapened Sedona. "New Age is very parasitic schtick," she says with characteristic certainty. "Everyone has services to share, but they're all for sale. Many young people live here with private trusts. To be a starving artist these days, you need a private income."

Rob Bell, who listens intently to others as they speak, agrees that New Age hasn't done Sedona any favors. "New Agers are far bigger here than most people think. Shops open all the time. It's an economic factor here. We've become the alternative medicine capital of the world. There's an alternative therapist on every corner offering medical services. I wouldn't trust one of them."

Unlike some communities, where different groups resort to nasty notes under windshields, Sedona residents don't let their beliefs lead to rudeness.

"I've never met anyone who lives here who is judgmental or unkind about New Age," says Concetta, who moved to Sedona a few years ago.

A vibrant woman with Catherine Zeta-Jones looks, she does massage therapy and psychic readings. After surviving a Brown Recluse spider bite that was pronounced fatal, she walked away from her life in national marketing. As a metaphysical bookstore was near her office, she'd been learning for 10 years from books she bought on her lunch hour. She began studying massage as a first step to Reiki therapy, an ancient Asian form of healing. "I wanted to make the rest of my life worth living," she says. "My spirit guides told me to move to Sedona, and I didn't even know where it was! I don't think anyone who knew me five years ago would even recognize me now."

Concetta loves the community, New Age and otherwise. "You see a huge number of tremendously loving people here," she says. "I do see some who sell land, and build, and want money, but I don't have a problem with it. Our community is big enough for people with lots of different goals. If you're really following your path, you can't get caught up with what others are doing."

Sara Junz works at the Center for the New Age in Sedona. A blonde woman with a keen assessing gaze and temperate voice, she does mostly psychic readings, but loves the occasional client who requests regression hypnosis or advice from the archangel Michael, whom she says she channels.

"A lot of people I get have never had psychic readings, and I consider it an honor to work with them," she says. "Sedona has quite a dichotomy of people. Some love the hills and build big houses on them. Others are New Age. I don't know any of the first group personally, but I've only lived here two years." Junz believes Sedona ranks with Taos and Santa Fe in New Mexico, Boulder, Colorado and Austin, Texas as sites for those seeking psychic wisdom and healing. She says that the irony is like that of people coming west to escape their allergies and then plant trees full of pollen; for every person who finds peace, it makes it harder for some psychics to practice their art because, "they leave their old negative energy here." She says. "So I need to get out of Sedona sometimes; I feel much more grounded and calmer other places."

Mahoney believes that as Sedona's New Age stock rises, its artistic image wanes. "Serious collectors don't come here any more," she says. "They go to L.A. I've taken my Sedona address off all my publicity material because it's the kiss of death. It's thought of as amateur or tourist art."

Not everyone agrees. Driving in from Interstate 17, galleries line both sides of the road, with dramatic sculptures and carvings beguiling the eye. Against the background of nature's sculptures, these metal and bronze works are not diminished, but aesthetically enhanced. From certain points in town, Sedona still shows off its beauty. Many areas are tucked away, so development doesn't show until you're almost upon it. It is possible to get caught up in the improbable cliffs carved and buffed by time, and the juxtaposition of color – deep green enfolding the creek, sienna and spice above, with the mantle of cerulean beyond.

While Larry Green says that the setting of rusty rock against impossibly blue skies continues to delight him, he agrees he doesn't like the town Sedona has become. "My first impression of Sedona was that it was an ugly little town in the most beautiful place in the world."

Ironically, he believes the beauty of Oak Creek Canyon has killed it.

People who come, who see the light, decide to stay. Too many. "Developers come, and develop things. They come in and say, 'This place is a gold mine,' and invest money for a short time. They know they'll take cash out and go back to L.A. I was on a board to create an architectural plan. I called it 'The Builders' and Realtors' Full Employment Act.' It protected nothing but the right for them to do whatever they wanted here."

Yet there seems to be a disconnect between almost all the residents coming here by choice (few are descended from old families; most have been here less than ten years) and the helplessness many seem to feel about how the town grows. One might argue that as former CEOs, retirees, people successful enough to be able to afford to live here, these residents should easily command skills to steer growth in an acceptable manner.

"Developer" is uttered here like one might have said "Papist" in Elizabethan England. Artists, business people and volunteers seem overwhelmed by what real estate operations have done to their beloved Canyon. But when told that public opinion trumps money every time if it is mobilized, many shake their heads.

Patty Fox is a refreshing exception to the defeated and disenfranchised. One of the original residents, she holds two rather surprising beliefs: one, that not much has changed; and two, that things aren't actually so bad.

Fox is the widow of beloved Arizonan Kel Fox, who served in the State Legislature and the Land Department, as well as running the family ranching enterprises in Northern Arizona. Patty moves like a young girl, slim and straight and healthy from years of enjoying the outdoors. Her dramatic Indian jewelry has the patina of years and activity, like its wearer. Eyes full of intelligence are framed by a fan of tanned lines. A volunteer at the Sedona Historical Museum, a seamstress, tennis player and hostess, Patty says that even after six years, the absence of her husband is as keenly felt as when he died. "They say the memories help," she says, "but they're actually the problem. I can't go anywhere around here without seeing something we did or someplace we shared." Patty has come full circle by living in the Village of Oak Creek – an area known as Big Park when the Foxes moved their cattle there from Schnebly Hill Road every year for grazing. When she arrived as a bride, not only was the nearest Laundromat in Cottonwood, but it had wringer washers and wooden tubs for rinsing.

She merrily recalls driving into Sedona to sell their week's cache of eggs every Saturday at the Oak Creek Store, then going next door to the Cowboy Club where they could enjoy a rare leisure afternoon buying beer with the egg money. In those days, the cliques didn't gravitate to different restaurants, because there was little choice. "The Rainbow's End was the only place to socialize."

Fox is philosophical about the growth she's seen in more than a half-century living here. "Kel always said it would happen," she says. "And, of course, new people want to take over and change things." She doesn't disapprove of anyone wanting to make changes; her only condemnation is for those who move here and then want to close the gates behind them. And she shakes her head over people who still staunchly insist that water is not a problem.

Not only has the population exploded in Sedona, but the continuing drought reaches almost beyond anyone's memory. Fox misses the long monsoon season and abundant rain of the mid-20th century. "It would cloud over in the afternoon, and rain at around four," she says, "Then you'd have an hour or two when it stopped to dry diapers before dark. Then it would rain again at night – a deep soaking rain. Kel called it a grass rain."

Patty sighs. She is stoic about accepting what is, but you can see in the clear blue eyes memories of other times. As resolute as she is, she permits herself a moment to say, "I really miss the old days here."

At 43, Jackie Young doesn't remember the good old days, but doesn't think the current years will be recalled in the same way. One of a minority of non-retired working professionals, she doesn't feel nurtured by the community. It is the retired residents she blames. "The beauty here is healing, but it's a town without a heart," she says.

It isn't hard to get a consensus that Oak Creek would be better off with limited human impact; that if we could go back in time and make Sedona a national park like Bryce and Zion, we should. The shadows over the deep vistas can still take your breath away, but the eye has to edit out the foreground of paved roads and buildings. No matter how artfully the houses are painted to match the sandstone hues, they can be seen clearly.

Mahoney doesn't even approve of the cultural events that are presented here. "Actually it's inappropriate to have a cultural draw," she says. "People can go to San Francisco or Manhattan for that. This is a place just to be outdoors.

"It's inappropriate to live here," she goes on, warming up to her subject. "This isn't a place for humans or businesses or all the services a population needs. This is a place to visit, not to live."

Elizabeth Yancy agrees in concept.

"But I'm not giving my land back," she says with a rueful smile. "So what do we do? This is becoming a resort town, and we need to create a livable place and address the issues. We all think we know what's best. But the big questions are: what services should be provided, where is growth acceptable, and will there be water?"

Dixie Robeson doesn't have the answers to these questions, but is not plagued by them. A docent at the Sedona Historical Museum, she is surrounded by reminders of time passing, with ebb and flow. She doesn't worry about the future.

Giving credit to the new Mayor Pud Colquitt and others for taking the lessons learned from overdevelopment and preventing rampant growth in the future Robson says the town has endured "terrible growing pains" but has come through them with people far more dedicated to getting involved and making a difference.

And for anyone who has never before seen Sedona, the spectacular natural beauty still dominates the landscape. It isn't all gone. Driving up the switchbacks toward Flagstaff, the sweet spicy scent of the creek hasn't been overtaken by growth. The rare snowfall on the rock formations are a fantasy in their contrast of light and dark. Stars still seem to whirl overhead at night. Thunderstorms utilize the terrain to create mighty echoes of thunder like a bass turned high. The light still seduces the eye as it slides across the burnished rocks toward sunset.

Robeson gives special credit to the women in Sedona for taking up issues and causes, and seeing them through. Making the old Hart store the historical center of the community is one such project.

"It's being called the new Heart of Sedona." She smiles.

It is fitting that a town named after a woman who persevered through hard times, and demonstrated grace not by elegance, but by showing up for the day's measure of laundry and cooking and nursing, should have attracted women who also are willing to work. Determined women, willing to sew sunbonnets from Sedona Schnebly's pattern in order to raise money for the Historical Museum, willing to attend meetings and speak out, run for office and buck tradition.

Which isn't to leave out men: Sedona was named by a man, as a tribute to the woman he loved. T.C. Schnebly was one of the earlier settlers to come, and look, and realize this was a special place. He, too, leaves a legacy, as appropriate now as it was in the 1950's, which was hospitality. For T.C., that meant wandering downtown as a one-man Chamber of Commerce, introducing himself to visitors and suggesting interesting day trips. Now, it means welcoming visitors who want to gaze about, see and be stirred by the colors and patterns of nature.

Also part of the hospitality is preserving the legacy of Sedona's natural beauty – taking the stewardship of sandstone and sky seriously. More than any before it, this generation of Sedona residents has come, and seen the light; not only as it alters and embellishes the landscape, but also how people can make or break this landscape. It will be up to them to protect and preserve what they found when they came; to insure that those who come after will be still able to see that light.

PATTY FOX

JOELLA JEAN MAHONEY

STORMY SEDONA LANDSCAPE

AGRITOPIA FLAG

CHAPTER **18**

CREATED COMMUNITIES:
NEW URBANISM IN ARIZONA.

In Arizona, if you build it, they will come. Our weather, our open space, our abundant natural wonders and our comparatively low housing prices attract new residents by the thousands every month. The line that makes developers beam and conservationists shudder is "an acre an hour," referring to the speed at which open desert is being converted to structures.

While this pumps new workers and new paychecks into the economy, the bill at the other end is large. Water is regarded as a right, not a privilege. The "brown cloud" days increase from more pollution, and how to add the additional cars creates hot debate about transportation and freeways. Phoenix crept from sixth to fifth largest city in the United States during the past decade, and is closing in on fourth. For the most part, the Valley of the Sun is about sprawl: subdivisions off freeways, with strip malls to meet the residents' needs, warehouse stores strategically placed, and seemingly endless stucco and red roofing tile. It isn't always pretty, but it's ours.

Yet, some developers are responding to this by embracing New Urbanism, which in short is the concept of finding alternatives to sprawl. Town centers, pedestrian walkways, parks and front porches are some of the hallmarks of a New Urban plan. "Hybrids" are developments which incorporate aspects of a utopian New Urban town site into traditional limitations.

Partly because we still have large tracts of land, and freeways to get people there, Arizona has been drawing New Urban projects for almost 50 years, since the first retirement community broke ground in the West Valley. Green Valley followed, with Saddlebrooke and other retirement villages springing up in Southern Arizona. But this was just the beginning.

New Urbanism is about all the pluses of going backward with none of the minuses. Knowing your neighbors, but knowing you can jump on the 101 and be far away from them; walking to schools and parks but having your cell phone just in case; sitting on front porches without having to shell peas; we want Main Street, only with broadband, so that while the band practices in the gazebo we can check our email.

In Arizona, Anthem broke out in the 90's as a multi-age planned community. When Phoenicians first read about a town of up to 50,000 people to the north depending completely on Interstate 17, alarm rippled through those concerned with transportation issues. Sure enough, the traffic is horrible on that stretch of freeway. But to those who chose to move to Anthem, sitting in your car was a small price to pay for a chance to live in a manner unknown to the rest of the valley. The strict grid of Phoenix streets in neat rows makes driving and understanding directions a breeze, but is not conducive to a sense of community. Anthem embodies New Urbanism's goal of curving streets, cul de sacs and circle grids as ways of keeping people connected to one another and their neighborhoods. Schools within neighborhoods, green belts, and businesses restricted to certain areas brought shoppers in droves when Del Webb held its grand opening. With the motto, "Live, Work and Play," Anthem attracted people who wanted a different kind of place to call home.

Driving into Anthem off Interstate 17, one finds that the appeal is immediate: the huge water park and play land near the entrance, rippling fountains and rolling hills of grass. The community center, with its climbing wall and basketball courts, says "Picture yourself here" without a word. While the gated Country Club section holds the most expensive homes, the Parkside models can be almost 5,000 square feet, with stone arches and pools grand enough to prevent feeling second-class.

As it ages, Anthem's list of services grows. From a single Safeway, residents now have more than 20 restaurants and dozens of businesses from child care to pest control. Streets named "John Phillips Sousa Way", and "Inspiration," come off as either quintessentially American, or trying too hard.

But residents rave.

"As a Del Webb employee, I had a vision of what this could do for residents," says Bonnie Smith, a title worker. "There was a lot of excitement because it was multi-generational. 'Live, work and play' became a reality, and I'm living that dream!"

Marion Teisan agrees. She left Scottsdale because during the years since she moved there it became too congested. She likes knowing that the natural contours of the land around Anthem will prevent solid gridlock. "This is off the beaten path," she says. "Everything is here except Costco and Trader Joe's. We have an excellent builder. We're staying."

This was not the original plan. "We were actually on our way to Vegas to look at homes, and stopped here on the way. Up there just didn't compare. Once you saw Anthem, there was no way to live anywhere else."

Pat Henson vigorously agrees. She was in the habit of building a custom home, selling and moving on, and planned to do so again. Her first few years in Arizona were spent on the Hopi reservation, and wide-open space became a habit. Most land she looks at with an eye to building seems likely to be crowded in the next few years." But now I'm used to the deer, the javelina, the bobcats," she says. "And my neighborhood is so culturally diverse. I love it here."

She likes the commonality of Parkside, but the Country Club has its supporters; the clubhouse, with restaurant and huge patio, whispers that your next party could be here. Bill and Carol Engler chose the Country Club when Bill retired and moved from Maryland.

"Bill's job took us to many different states," says Carol. "I chose Arizona years ago, because family is here. I'd been looking in Scottsdale, but we got so much more home here than we could there. I'm used to tract homes, and we've never had so many options. You can really customize your home here, inside and out; you don't have to look like the house next door."

"We're active with the senior group," adds Bill. "The fees are high, but the amenities require that. We'll stay as long as we can take care of the house. Everything is here."

Not everyone plans to stay. Beatrix Wagner, a striking woman in her 20's, lives here with her boyfriend.

"At first I was afraid everyone would be families," she says. "But the essentials are here. Still, we're so far away from everything. I want acreage and a custom home, which we can't do here. And there aren't many people in their 20's. Still, if I were retired, or had children, it would be perfect."

Deborah Addleman, the mother of a high school son, is a little more reserved. She and her husband had a window of opportunity to move before their son started as a freshman, and chose Anthem after considering other locations, including Hawaii.

"We loved Hawaii, but couldn't afford anything," she says. "Here we could get a nice house, plus a pool, and still have money. But we didn't research schools enough. The system isn't what we expected, and there isn't much to do because being in the Teen club isn't cool. That's the biggest disappointment so far."

But three mothers of high school sons sharing iced tea on the country club patio after a tennis clinic, disagree. "We love the high school," says Marguerite Halbig, a vivacious blond with an infectious laugh. "They have honors classes, band, football, dances. Any new school has glitches, but some of the teachers live nearby, and there are girls' soccer games, and drama. Plenty to do!"

"The community has everything," agrees Mary Dill. "You make your own life. If you can't find something to do here, it's your own fault."

She uses her mother as an example; after moving in, her mother was hesitant about going to a senior citizens' group event.

"But she went, and she loves it! She's a Golden Go-Getter, and does volunteer work at the high school, and parties with the Red Hatters. It's been great."

Lynn Higgins agrees the high school is still getting geared up, and looks forward to when a movie theater opens on the west side of Interstate 17, so teenagers won't have to drive the freeway to Deer Valley for movies. But she knows until Anthem is built out, businesses are reluctant to invest in infrastructure. "When it sells out, they'll come in," she says. "I'll be happy to see more development closer to Anthem."

When Anthem residents get together, the subject of Vistancia invariably comes up. The new planned community to the west is being watched with interest and a little insecurity, as each fresh display of New Urbanism can learn from mistakes of the existing ones and retool. No one here admits to wanting to move, but many have taken tours just to see it.

The adage, "Wherever you go, there you are" prevents New Urban communities from being only the positive aspects of a small town. No screening process exists to prevent mean or immoral people from moving in, no matter how safe you want to feel. One Phoenix woman says the other family from her neighborhood to relocate to Anthem was the only one police had been called for domestic violence. Another says it would be Stepfordian to have no one under poverty level anywhere in sight. Sour grapes, perhaps. Some people prefer a beach vacuumed free of seaweed; others don't. But New Urban residents would be the first to say that if the lifestyle doesn't appeal, don't move there. Anthem is about choice.

One of the shortfalls of New Urbanism as played out in Arizona so far is the factor no builder can control: the free market. Businesses build where they please. So while the Interstate 10 corridor that houses Estrella Mountain Ranch and Verrado hopes manufacturing will be attracted, and believes Westcor's biggest mall ever will break ground nearby, all the new towns struggle to provide sufficient services that the residents want. And while some Anthem residents work at home, or commute at odd hours, many complain bitterly about tie-ups on the freeway, as if they had nothing to do with causing the problem. Together, they can't seem to stop discussing various ways of getting around the clogged stretch of Interstate 17 into Phoenix.

Residents are loyally reluctant to address the idea that Anthem is elitist. Off the record, one says, "The only Mexicans you see here are working in yards." Another shakes his head about what he ruefully dubs "The Asian Invasion," where absentee landlords rent out homes they've purchased. Beyond garage thefts, none has heard of any rapes or assaults. Sirens are almost always for medical emergencies, not crimes. To some extent, you can carpet the kingdom.

On the opposite end of the Valley of the Sun is Agritopia, the brainchild of a man named Joe Johnston, who sold about 200 acres to Scott Builders to create his dream. Based again on the small-town model, Agritopia will stop far short of Anthem's 50,000 people. It's meant to be small enough that everyone truly can know your name; the public gardens that put the "agri" in "utopia" beckon to people who will be able to inquire after one another's families and discuss school sports. A farmer's market is a weekly event to bring people together and help them appreciate the bounty of the earth.

Homes have a postwar Midwestern influence, as if a Frank Capra film might be unfolding on the next street. While the homes are not large, basement options making six and seven bedrooms possible flag Agritopia as a haven for religious families with many children.

One striking difference between Agritopia and other New Urban developments is its calm disclosure up front that this is a community based on Christian values. The Agritopia website states that the Johnston brothers "believe that Creation, the fall of man, and the plan of salvation through Jesus Christ are real."

While it goes on to say that "no one can be made or coerced into being a Christian by other people," and that "all people are welcome in this community," it is a buffer between the complicated real world, where school children must learn about Eid and Ramadan, and the selective reality of a planned community.

Joe Johnston speaks freely about his mission statement. After making a comfortable fortune with his wildly successful Coffee Plantation chain in the Valley, Johnston believes that no one can truly succeed without applying Christian principles to any endeavor. He says he has no idea what religious affiliation the Agritopia residents are, but knows that not all are Christian. He is proud of the way the community is growing, and says having studied lots of other developments gave his group the insight to start doing things right from the beginning. Agritopia has gaining attention for creating a "no renters" policy to avoid the problem of absentee landlords that troubles some Anthem residents.

New planned communities keep cropping up. Heading west on I-10 from the Valley, you wonder if Verrado is really there. Desert runs into mountains with no discernible buildings even as you take the Verrado exit.

But follow the new and winding road and you pull around to a surprising sight: a civilized, even elegant community truly in the middle of nowhere, although near the foothills of the White Tanks Mountains. Over time this will change as businesses and hotels creep ever outward from Estrella and Goodyear, but for now it is an oasis of optimism and newness.

Each planned community has the luxury of learning from those who have gone before. Verrado, for example, has avoided the numbing sameness of beige and stucco. When Verrado boasts varied architecture, it delivers.

Ten builders incorporate certain constants with seemingly unlimited variety. With all the models and elevations, it seems possible no two homes would turn out the same. All true to the southwestern archetype, Spanish Colonial, Ranch Territorial, Craftsman, and Regional Farmhouse elements both blend and stand out. Historic homes in Phoenix neighborhoods were studied for inspiration. The models are a buffet of abundant charm: varied rooflines, intriguing courtyards and balconies, front porches and wide welcoming terraces. Even detractors of planned communities, with their careful culling out of the wrong element and isolation from diversity, can be beguiled by the gabled roofs and pillared patios. Neighborhoods were set out in a purposeful but seemingly random pattern, with the plan being that residents can say they live near the school, downtown, the wash, or the golf club, as one would in an organically evolved village. But along with elaborate molding, roofs of tile, shingle and metal, and traditional architecture, these old-fashioned neighborhoods come with high-speed Internet access, web portal access and bi-directional video capability built in, and no antique wiring to replace. It would take a strong person to walk down the wide, tree-shaded streets knowing that this deep porch with the Spanish tile could be yours, and choose instead the faceless anonymity of a tract neighborhood just for a higher chance of having your children could grow up with diversity.

Verrado is drawing retirees, young couples and families at a seemingly equal rate, offering larger lots for big houses, the convenience of closer homes, and the luxury of the golf club and course. Everything is brand new, and exacting homeowners' associations and deed restrictions will keep the town as fresh and pretty as it is today.

Another feature of planned communities is a business district, which at Verrado plays out as the Main Street District. Designers looked at classic downtowns, like Palo Alto, California and Savannah, Georgia before they began drawing. A more appealing town center doesn't exist, with the two-story buildings lining Main Street, all as sparkling and welcoming as the one in Disneyland. "Wine shop," "grocery," "coffee," promise the signs, with outdoor seating a further enticement to shop. Over the businesses are lofts that can be rented but never purchased, for those who truly want to feel the pulse of the community.

At one end of the main street, a flagpole and fountain flank a mission-style building that houses the Village Club, where residents can congregate for sports and play. The whole place feels like a movie set, with the knowledge that you, too, could be in the cast if you bought one of the elegantly detailed homes. Overall the impression is of a dream small town, brand new and waiting to be enjoyed.

All this comes with only one tradeoff: the real world. There is little economic or cultural diversity here. There is simply a slight unreal quality to it.

New Urbanism is not for everyone. But it's interesting to note that what people yearn for is what they fled from fifty years ago: small towns.

It will be fascinating to see over the course of the next generation what other aspects of small town life spring out of New Urban centers. Will the village raise the children, so that parents get a call if their teenager is rude in traffic or commits vandalism? Will neighbors grow tired of everyone knowing what car they drive and where it was parked?

Will cliques form as surely as they did in earlier small towns, with people trapped in their parents' reputations? Or will the finer aspects of small town life emerge: places where people live with loyalty to their town and affection for their fellow residents? It's reassuring, somehow, to know that front porches and parks and a main street touch something deep inside us. A desire, after all, to be included, be known. Belong.

ANTHEM

VERRADO TOWN SQUARE

CATHY GOSHERT

CHAPTER 19

VALLEY OF THE SUN

Maricopa County is an irony to some Arizonans. While about two-thirds of the state's population resides there, most of what Arizona is known for lies outside the county boundaries. While the Grand Canyon, Sedona, Indian Country, Tombstone, San Xavier Mission, Lake Powell, are far-flung in distance, many decisions affecting them are made in Maricopa County at the State Capitol.

On the other hand, the resorts, golf courses and conference centers in Maricopa County generate a sizable chunk of the state's revenue. The "Valley of the Sun" houses the fifth-largest city and sixth-largest airport in the United States. It is an area that is geographically similar but widely diverse in residents.

From the new retirees moving into Surprise to the old Hispanic families in Guadalupe, the population of the Valley of the Sun is as colorful as, some say, the desert landscape is monotone. Unlike small towns, the cities that comprise the Valley are more difficult to sum up in one comprehensive portrait. So this section is made up of five vignettes of individuals selected from around the Valley, each one a voice in the symphony of residents who call it home. A teacher from a family of educators in Phoenix, three young professionals from Scottsdale, a businessman from Awahtukee, a mother from Mesa and an attorney from South Phoenix are the individuals who highlight a few aspects of what it means to them to be a Valley resident.

PHOENIX: PAST AND FUTURE

About 140 years ago, Valley of the Sun founding father, Darrell Duppa, suggested to fellow founding father Jack Swilling that their fledgling-community be named not Stonewall for Stonewall Jackson, but Phoenix, for the fact that this town would rise like a phoenix from the ashes of a Hohokam site dating back to 1000 A.D.

Now, in the center of the massive metropolis of Phoenix, at Mercury Mine Elementary School, a Hohokam site is again rising in a patch of desert.

Cathy Goshert looks at the piece of the desert under her stewardship and sighs. As leader of Mercury Mine Elementary School's Desert Dudes group, she is in charge of a layout of structures and walkways on the school's property. Today's job is recreating the vandalized Pima kitchen made of saguaro ribs, this time using rebar and wire to better withstand another destructive attack. Over the years successive groups of Desert Dudes have cleared pathways, bordered them with rock, constructed a pit house, and created displays of matates and other simple tools that previous cultures who populated this area once used. Goshert and her family have been preparing the standing posts so that Desert Dudes can lay the saguaro ribs between them to form walls. Goshert, a petite blonde with wiry grace, hands out tools and explains the job ahead.

At first it's a bit like herding cats: a large group of students out of school for the day tend to catch up on things of more current interest before applying themselves to the task at hand. But the better workers begin dragging sticks and branches from the pile right away, and gradually the chatter subsides as the rest see actual results from their labor.

Goshert's mother, Glenda Pershing, is a retired Mercury Mine teacher, and one of the visionaries behind creating this place, the Desert Education Center. Although the traffic from the Squaw Peak Parkway hums nearby, the hilly area filled with creosote and mesquite seems removed from the city. The hope is that through their efforts, these children in work gloves will develop an appreciation and awareness of both the area in which they live, and the heritage of the Desert People, from a thousand years past to the present time.

Of course, any teacher knows that results won't be calculated until decades after the effort has been spent. So whether the students poking cautiously into the pile of cactus ribs will become environmental advocates and cultural leading lights is not now determinable. But today, they are involved in preservation, stabilization and cultural awareness.

Leading this group isn't just a hobby. Education is a load-bearing beam in Goshert's life. Her mother, aunt, and mother-in-law are teachers. With a master's degree in education, she is on leave from Paradise Valley School District to raise her four children. This is one outlet for teaching; another is substituting in her mother's class at Mercury Mine – which includes her youngest son and daughter. Her two older sons are alumni of their grandma's classroom. All this is to say that in a city where two people move out for every three who move in, Goshert is an anomaly – a deeply rooted Phoenician with branches on the family tree spreading across the Valley. Both she and her husband Brett grew up here. Both sets of their parents still live here. All of the couple's siblings live here – as well as her sister's in-laws, his sister's in-laws, and many cousins. They are an extended family that would do any Midwestern town proud, but they are local through and through. Goshert remembers when Metrocenter opened, watching Wallace and Ladmo, and when Brett was her swim coach for the city Parks and Rec summer program.

Pausing between helping two boys wrestle a particularly unwieldy length of saguaro into place and calling another errant Desert Dude back to task, Goshert ruefully surveys the work. "Even if we don't finish today, I hope they feel they had a real part in this." Between teaching, and raising four active and involved children, she has had to learn how to shoot for the stars and accept the shortfalls. She shares the secret life of most contemporary mothers – meals in the car between appointments and pickups, schedules snarled by students who forget to bring home slips for field trips or need projects dropped off, always the wistful belief that somewhere in the chaos are the seeds of creating a better world by giving children opportunities and experiences.

For her family and their relatives, Phoenix is a good cultural fit: There are fine museums, theaters, restaurants (she knows all the child-friendly ones) and many outdoor activities. And like family, Phoenix is neither good or bad – it simply is accepted, flaws and all. But asked what she likes about her hometown, Goshert speaks with an appreciative sense of place, "The smell of the desert when it rains, the weather in February, orange blossoms, and monsoons."

Goshert's home indicates an emphasis on education: books and board games in most rooms, photographs and souvenirs from trips overseas with various family members. This is the house where animals from classrooms come to spend their summer vacations, where end-of-year parties fill the house, yard and pool with teeming exuberance. Family gatherings have been Roman feasts and Lord of the Rings festivals complete with costumes. Goshert makes surprise pancakes for April Fools Day and roast goose for Christmas. Her days revolve around bringing as many experiences to life as she can for her family, from Shakespeare to making jelly from the prickly pear in their front yard.

Spend any time at Goshert's house, and the twin priorities of family and education are consistent: the sisters car-pool to one grandma's class at Mercury Mine; the other grandmother comes over to tutor in math. Cousins see one another not just at parties, but at school and on weekend sleepovers. Children are constantly rotating through the house as mothers move from getting together to make jewelry and crafts, to gathering a group to help at the Adobe Mountain Wildlife Center. It's a frenetic life, and Goshert may be too caught up in the swirl of activities to notice what she's created. But in the middle of a huge, impersonal city full of transitory residents and disconnected souls, she maintains a sanctuary – a home where generations gather, where security and curiosity co-exist, and learning means adventure as much as it does reading. By being willing to be the woman behind the pickax and the mother in the middle of the party, Goshert is helping create the future citizens of Phoenix, one child – or sometimes more – at a time.

SOUTH PHOENIX: BARRIO

You can take the boy out of the barrio, but he may well move back.

DANNY ORTEGA

"Barrios," Spanish-speaking neighborhoods that began springing up in Arizona in the 1870s, raised generations of children before urban renewal and downtown revitalization took their toll. The old adobe homes, with front walls up against the sidewalks, and courtyards in back, fell under wrecking balls starting in the 60s. A few still remain, and where they have disappeared, former residents have returned to the area and built new homes to be near the site of their childhood memories.

At least Danny Ortega did. Sitting in the boardroom of his law offices, Ortega could be anywhere – Beverly Hills, New York City. But just outside, the distinctive radio tower atop the historic Westward Ho building is silhouetted against the sky. Visible from almost anywhere in South Phoenix, it is a signal to Ortega that he is in the right place. He is home.

"I say I grew up in South Phoenix – we lived at 19th Avenue and Buckeye," he says. "But people who lived south of the Salt River say that's South Phoenix and that we grew up in the inner city. We don't think of it like that. To us, the barrio was South Phoenix."

The area is now part of downtown, but from one street to the next it bounces from businesses to blight. Some of the lovely, restored homes are offices. But other streets are places where many Phoenicians might feel uncomfortable leaving their cars. Even Ortega's office keeps the door locked during the day. Yet loyalty trumps location to Ortega, who lives and works close to his roots.

The oldest of eight siblings, when it came time to build his home, Ortega bought a lot within a mile of where he grew up. "And five — no, six in the family, live within a three-mile radius," he says proudly. Ortega's crisp white shirt may be the mark of a successful businessman, but he wears it as casually as he would denim. Over 50, his ebullient face is that of a much younger man, brimming with enthusiasm for what the day may offer, and joy at discovering more of an interesting world.

He swears his story is common: a Spanish-speaking couple from El Paso moving the family to South Phoenix, where the father worked in the fields, and later moved up to driving trucks while the mother stayed home.

"She was a natural leader, a do-what-you've-got-to-do person," states Ortega. He seems to enjoy describing the early years when whatever fruit or produce somehow separated from his fathers' delivery load would be brought home to sell door-to-door.

"My mother would pile us into the old Rambler, driving melons down the street," he says. "Fifty cents each, or three for a dollar. My sister Hilda was four; when she asked, everything would sell. So I would just stand next to her at the door." But he never felt poor.

"We were economically disadvantaged, but we were rich in culture, rich in love," he insists. "Did the roof leak? Yes. Were the utilities turned off? Yes. Did the welfare truck drive up to the front of our house? Yes. But we always had what we needed."

He laughs remembering that his mother would say, "We're poor, but we're not pigs." "We were clean. We swept the house, we swept the yard. We watered down the dirt!"

Now, in Ortega's office a receptionist brings us coffee and the furnishings gleam. Still, he denies that his success is special. "There are literally thousands of families just like ours," he says. "Families where we were the first generation who learned English and went to college. And we did well. But the pride comes from the togetherness. If you teach your kids respect, and hard work, the rest takes care of itself."

Asked how the boy who started school speaking only Spanish rose to the level of a highly regarded attorney and activist, Ortega answers, "There's no secret. I grew up surrounded by people who loved me – all my life."

Maybe the support from home was what kept Ortega from giving up when he was held back in first grade. Spanish was spoken at home, and he didn't catch on to English quickly enough to move with the class to second grade.

It was Mrs. Cummings in second grade who took the time to bring the boy along. "I still remember her," he says, earnestly. "She cared so much! I can't even remember now not being able to communicate." From then on, it never occurred to Ortega that limits existed. He laughs that the only time it ever dawned on him he might not get through law school was when he got his grades back the first year. But again, the natural self-confidence carried him through. Now he gives back to his community by being a requested speaker on Hispanic and border issues.

"The more I give, the more I want to give," he says. "I feel I have more than I should have anyway. I think this a lot of the time." So he operates on the edge of politics and current events, addressing groups around the state. The lines drawn between races and cultures disturb him. "Lines divide, and create hatred," he says. "And I know hatred comes from fear. People have always feared newcomers – the Irish, the Germans. Now, it's the Muslims, the Arabs. We have to see groups are different. Then let it go."

Ortega looks again to the barrio for examples, and finds them in the people he calls "the unsung heroes of our generation." "These are the people who do church ministries, conduct Bible study for a neighborhood," he says, "People who go pick up grandma and take her to the store. People who drop by the neighbor's with dinner because they know there's no food. They make as big a difference as the Congressman who gets millions for his district. The sphere of influence is different, but the giving is the same. And maybe more, because they have so little to begin with."

Now that his three children are successfully raised, Ortega has a new goal. He clearly takes pride in the fact that his children treasure the extended family he stays here for."We still get together for holidays – all the aunts and uncles and cousins," he says. "Now, our children, too. That's what matters." He looks reflective. "I could lose all my money tomorrow – a bad business decision," he says. "And now that I've had it, I would miss it. But I would be okay. Because the togetherness, the love, would still be there." Which is what the barrio gave him. Which is why it's still home.

Scottsdale Plaza

SCOTTSDALE: THE BIGGEST SMALL TOWN

More than a century ago, Army Chaplain Winfield Scott came across a gentle landscape near Phoenix and fell in love with it. In a move that would make developers today weep, he paid $2.50 per acre for the area now bordered by Chaparral on the north, Hayden on the east, Indian School on the south and

Scottsdale Road on the west. He invited his brother George out west to take charge of clearing, fencing and planting the area with citrus, barley and grapes. The tent George Scott pitched at what is now the intersection of Indian School and Scottsdale Road made him the first official resident of his namesake, Scottsdale.

As time brought more residents to the area, the crops gave way to homes. Far before most communities thought about beautification, Scottsdale passed a strict sign ordinance that put it at the forefront of urban planning. Resorts and golf courses were laid out to welcome tourists, galleries and a lovely Civic Plaza enchanted them. The town charmed tourists, who then became residents, gaining Scottdale a reputation as one of the West's loveliest destination towns.

Mention Scottsdale and people think of golf courses, resorts sprawled across the foothills of Camelback Mountain. But to some, downtown defines the city, with the western shop fronts along the narrow avenues, the Pink Pony for ice cream, and the lawns and white sculptures outside the Scottsdale Museum of Modern Art.

On a late afternoon, in spring, at the Scottsdale Civic Plaza, blossoms flutter and the grass is an almost decadent shade of green. Bird songs and light breezes take turns dancing with water music from the fountains and lake. It's a pastoral performance witnessed by an occasional passer-by and diners on the postmodern white chairs of the AZ88 patio. A traditional meeting place for city workers, young professionals, and the theater crowd, the sleek architecture and insouciant furnishings embody the sophisticated ease that is Scottsdale.

Three of these young professionals are here to interpret their town for us. Cassidy Campana, an energetic blond with outgoing manners and subtle makeup, is a public relations director and a native. Kurt Merschman is a corporate attorney evocative of Matt Damon, and David Barnett is a broker with a low-key manner. Both men have lived here for eight years.

Asked to explain what Scottsdale is like, the three start a conversation which twice includes, "Oh, I know her." Merschman smiles. "This is a perfect example of what it's like here," he says. "You begin talking and even if you haven't lived here that long, it's amazing how many people you both know."

Campana nods. "This is the biggest small town in America," she says. "I was born here, and I really do think of it as my community. It's strange, though – I also pulled in most of my college friends. They'd visit, then they'd move here."

The three speakers have a lot in common: all are professionals who traveled around Europe before living in Washington, D.C., and finally moving to Arizona.Campana cites the contrast between living in D.C. and Scottsdale.

"You can get involved here. It's not like the East Coast, where you have to be from a certain family to be included. Here, it's merit based." She says that if you're interested in community service, the way to get in is to know one of about 150 people who make up the town's inner circle. Barnett counters that it's more like one of 75 people.

"The good thing is that you don't have to do twenty years of service before you can get involved. There is a very tight community of people who know everybody, but once you connect with one of those, you're in."

"The city is very welcoming to people who want to get involved," Merschman agrees. "Maybe because of the population boom, you can't help but allow new people in, because the growth overwhelms the natives. And that's not a bad thing."

As the population grows, the grip of the Old Guard is loosened, yet the three agree that Charros still hold a certain cache. This is the group of men who engage in service club activities, and also hold rides for members and guests. Merschman mentions being invited on a ride, and is asked if he wants to be a member. He laughs. "If you want to be in, you'll never get in."

While they have much in common, the three have chosen different aspects of Scottsdale to call home. Campana loves the rural horse country and openness of North Scottsdale, and cites the 36 miles of horse trails as a huge plus. She thinks even more would be better. Merschman chose a neighborhood that he says reminds him of the small town where he grew up in Iowa. "It's very similar to the Midwest in terms of community," he says. "It's very much about the people. Maybe it's just my circle, but eight out of ten people I know are from the Midwest. On my street, people fly Michigan flags, and do football Saturdays."

Barnett chose an older home on an acre lot in North Scottsdale, and marvels at a city that affords young professionals that kind of purchase, compared to friends in San Diego or D.C. who barely manage their condo payments. "It's remarkable that in a city this size, we can have a conversation about how many miles of horse trails is appropriate," he adds.

As a broker, Barnett keeps abreast of demographic trends, and notices a shift back toward downtown from the previous surge north. "Some people who bought up in Troon when it opened are either moving back, or buying a second town home or loft down here. They move back for the availability of the luxury life without the drive," Merschman says. And Campana adds that the newest boom is small boutique hotels rather than large spread out resorts. "There's one on the corner here," she says. "People want to walk to dinner, to clubs, to shopping."

Asked what Barnett wants his life to be like in 20 years, he smiles. "Just a grownup version of where we are already. I think the city would benefit from a little more contribution from the younger, techie crowd, but other than that, it's all here."

Campana says Scottsdale is a great place, but maybe a little on the sterile side. "It could use more funkiness," she says. "Actually, the sterility is attractive to me," counters Merschman. "It's a running joke in our group that you never go farther west than Central or east past Tempe. I could count on one hand the times I go outside that corridor. I consider myself open-minded, and I love good restaurants. But I don't have to leave Scottsdale to get all I want."

THE FAULKNER FAMILY OF MESA

MESA: FAMILY ROOM

Some 125 years ago, the Mormons were the first residents in what is now Mesa; the Church of Jesus Christ of Latter-day Saints sent out parties from Salt Lake City to colonize empty – and therefore safe – terrain in Arizona. One advantage in getting to plot the town before building it was that all original roads were 130 feet wide – big enough for a horse team and wagon to turn around easily. Today that space is more likely to be enjoyed by lumbering SUVs, with mothers transporting children to school, soccer or Scouts. Mesa is still a bastion for large Mormon families.

Side by side with them is a significant population of Hispanics. Catholic parents are drawn to the same large houses and child-friendly atmosphere as are the Latter Day Saints. Parts of Mesa have experienced a type of white flight as prosperous working couples move to shiny new homes going up in Gilbert or Chandler. Some Mesa schools struggle with the majority of students who speak only Spanish at home. This not only strains a system forbidden to use Spanish in the classroom, but creates hardships for the Anglo students who are unable to move ahead faster than those who are still learning English.

But because Mesa is what it is, residents of the new estate-size homes don't resent or ignore the less affluent living nearby.

Kim Faulkner opens the door at the end of the hall to a suite of rooms large enough to house in-laws or teenagers – indeed, it was her grandmother's until she moved in with another relative. Now, this is where Kim and other mothers gather to quilt and sew for the less fortunate. She collects diapers, Christmas baskets and other supplies in here, and her face glows describing the pleasure she takes in gathering teenage girls for afternoons of sewing, teaching and laughter.

This is not out of need to fill an empty home or life – her own six children rocket around the house with cousins, friends, and copious energy. But Faulkner is the kind of woman most others marvel at: a mother and wife with seemingly inexhaustible stores of nurturing and caring.

"I still can't quite believe this is the last baby," she says over the head of Cailee, whose corn silk head bobs after waking from a nap. "But we almost have too many birthdays. It finally came to me that we're done. And I am excited to move on to the next stage." In the spacious living room, 12-year-old Torie practices the piano, 11-year-old Greyson is building a model in his room, Aubrey, at 9, has cousins to play with, five-year-old Ethan rides his bike in the back yard, and Dallin, three, huddles close to his mother, but seems to have only tenderness, not envy, toward the baby being held.

Faulkner dismisses her humanitarian aid work as if it is something anyone would do. "It's not real prestigious to be Humanitarian Leader, it's just a job. But we do get a lot of quilts and clothes, and you can see results for your work." Her household is elastic – cousins and children's friends are included at mealtime with no more than a head count. They gather around the picnic table in the family room more often than they carry plates into the elegant dining room. From her giant pantry, Faulkner effortlessly creates a snack, drawing from bulk containers of pretzels, dried fruits and huge containers of juice. She says she loves the frenetic activity, and she must mean it, for not many could stand it for long, otherwise. Her wide blue eyes crinkle with amusement at the idea that adding a dozen guests overnight is not normal in most homes.

"I think sometimes these are the best years of our lives," she says. "But then I look at women at church who have a dozen grandchildren coming over every Sunday, and I think that might be at least as good as this."

Like many parents, she worries about over-scheduling her brood.

You can get so involved with activities that you pull the family apart," she says earnestly. "In the world today, it's really hard to be sensible, because there are so many choices, so many things to get involved in. But you really have to be careful to keep it in check." She describes the huge calendar that tracks everyone's activities, and the smaller version she takes with her for making appointments.

Kim says they religiously keep Family Home Evening, where everyone gathers for teaching, prayer and activities together. And they seek out experiences to participate inas a group, instead of each child going to separate practices or games. They visit the Temple every Christmas for the light display that draws thousands to the spacious grounds, and go to the pageant at Easter. "We all went to a President's Day celebration," she says, "They had people dressed up as Founding Fathers, and the children got to sign a 'Declaration of Independence.' There was so much to enjoy!"

Faulkner's husband Mark is a Battalion Chief with the Phoenix Fire Department. Genial, seeming unruffled among the bustle of ten children having fun, he clearly admires his wife's ability to maintain the priority of family and faith in a larger world. And rather than worry about having enough money to keep the empire running, the couple is concerned about having too much.

"Actually, we don't have as much as many of our neighbors," says Faulkner. "But most everyone has too much! We don't have racial tension here – there's a huge population of Hispanics, and our school has students bussed from the Gila Reservation. Everyone gets along. But the problems you see around here are kids with so much money and fast cars, it leads to decisions that aren't the best. They can buy drugs. Kids who are given everything, and expect to get it without working. We had a problem at another school because they were bringing home candy every day as a reward. That's too much."

Now, the school-age Faulkners go to a back-to-basics school Each plays a musical instrument. The parents try to limit after-school activities to one sport at a time. And Faulkner says she applies the same reins to her own schedule.

"Even as an adult, there are so many things I can spend my time on. But I don't want to spread myself so thin I don't do my most important job. Mostly, I want to raise wonderful children, productive members of our society. I want to leave a legacy I can be proud of."

Seeing the small heads bowed for grace in the family room, it doesn't seem too much to expect.

VADA, ADA, CHARLENE MANAGER

AHWATUKEE: HOUSE OF DREAMS

Nestled in the foothills of South Mountain Preserve, Ahwatukee is named for a ranch built there in the 1920s. It was the second owner, Helen Brinton who christened it Ahwatukee, which is "House of Dreams" in Crow language. While no Crow Indians lived here, others did. Initially they hunted and farmed. Later, gold and silver mines dotted the area. Now, it is made up of gated communities with sprawling homes for about 75,000 people. At least one, Vada Manager, has his House of Dreams.

Manager lives here despite being Global Issues Management Director for Nike, whose United States headquarters are in Oregon. Manager's staff is there, as well as in Beijing and Hong Kong, but to him it's worth the extra trips to Sky Harbor to be able to call Arizona home. While he was raised in East St. Louis, this is where Manager wants to raise his family. Walk into his backyard bordered on three sides by magnificent desert foothills, and it's clear enough that Manager's affection for the place includes the natural beauty. But to him, Arizona is home defined by people every bit as much.

Coming to Arizona State University as "a skinny 19-year-old," he says, he didn't know that becoming a Student Regent on the Arizona Board of Regents would be his entrée into Arizona's circle of power. But being raised by his mother, his grandparents and great-grandparents meant being a grown up sitting around the dinner table discussing everything from politics to human rights.

"Because of being raised with that level of adults per square foot, it was easy to walk up to a regent and say, 'This is what I think,' and they really took me under their wings," he says. Tall and lean, with early grey hair and a large laugh, Manager embodies Rudyard Kipling's line from the poem, "If," by being able "to walk with kings, nor lose the common touch." His experiences since college have included traveling to China with Michael Jordan, working with CNN at the Democratic National Convention, attending Olympics and meeting with Nelson Mandela in Africa. Still, he welcomes children to his home, offering them food, drink and entertainment as respectfully and attentive as if they were world leaders.

Manager seems to be able to be two complete people: one, the international strategist who operates out of what he calls "the nerve center," with computers, communications lines and a television for video conferencing until one or two in the morning. The other is devoted to family, taking his wife to Greece for the concluding ceremonies of the Olympics and a holiday in Crete, including his children on his trips to other countries, and looking forward to bringing his mother out from St. Louis again this year. He smiles talking about getting to be part of then-President Bill Clinton's trip to Viet Nam ("The first

United States presidential visit since the conflict"), and he gets equally enthu siastic talking about taking his children to Washington D.C. ("It's a great city! You have the Smithsonian, where all the riches of the world, all the great memories of our country are gathered, and it's all free – just walk through the door! So much knowledge, the wealth of intellect, and because of your, or your parents' tax dollars, it's available to everyone.")

While Manager fits the Ahwatukee profile of upper-management executive and family man, his experiences set him apart. After working as press aide for then-Governor and presidential candidate Bruce Babbitt, then for Governor Rose Mofford, Manager met and became friends with Washington D.C. Mayor Sharon Pratt Kelley and met Nelson Mandela. It was this meeting that led to Manager being part of a State Department team that was flown to Africa to help Mandela as the newly elected leader.

"You've got to remember that before transition, most of Mandela's administration had been underground revolutionaries or in prison." Manager says. "We took some of the cabinet to a small farm in Pretoria, to go over strategy, transition, to discuss working with reporters and speechwriting." It's clear this was a momentous event in Manager's life."Especially," he adds, "because as a youth in East St. Louis, I figured the only way I'd ever get to see the world was in uniform as a member of the armed services. Not everyone from my high school went to college." Somehow, despite his birthplace, Manager says he avoided the potential pitfalls others fell into, "I have never consumed a Bud. I've never had a cigarette. To be able to conduct the business I have, has been incredible. I never take it for granted."

As much as he loved Arizona, Manager said he might have been more comfortable choosing to live elsewhere. "Here, there was no one who looked like me sitting around boardrooms or executive suites," he says. "New York, Atlanta, Chicago would have offered more African American businessmen as role models." But his admiration and affection for people here prevailed. One thing he appreciates about Arizona is that "unlike some big cities, where you have to be from the right family or get in line, here if you have a work ethic and are willing to roll up your sleeves and jump in, you can get to a high level in your 20s."

He also says no matter where he has lived – Oregon, London, or D.C. — he kept subscriptions to the Arizona Republic and Arizona Informant. "I loved Phoenix so much I actually lived here in a mobile home for a while rather than move," he says with a broad smile. Now, he lives in a wide, welcoming home, with bedrooms for each of the five children, and a guesthouse that serves as a rec room with every game system known. Outdoors, besides the view, are a trampoline, a putting green and a basketball court.

During the conversation, Manager's wife, Charlene, arrives home with five-year-old Trent and Ada, almost a year old. The three older children made Vada a father when he married Charlene. Fourteen-year-old Marcus has already welcomed guests and helped set up GameCube; 20-year-old Elise and 16-year-old Garrett arrive from the airport after a weekend away. When Elise joins us on the patio, she and Charlene squeal, do a little happy dance and run to one another's arms. After meeting at ASU, Manager and Charlene stayed connected through friends – "I always knew he was okay, even if we didn't talk for a few years," she says. When they met again in the late 90s, Manager was thinking he was finally ready to consider marriage and a family. He had a four-bedroom house in Oregon. "So I had the right idea – just the wrong place," he says. A photograph in the entry hall shows the couple on their wedding day at L'Auberge in Sedona. As Ada snuggles into his arms, Manager watches Trent race over to the trampoline, and smiles.

"You know," he says. "I've worked with presidents, athletes and the media. But none of that compares to this – to being a father." This is, indeed, a house of dreams come true.

CHAPTER 20

CALLING ARIZONA HOME

"We shall cease from exploration
And the end of all our exploring
Will be to arrive where we started
And know the place for the first time"
"Little Gidding" T.S. Elliot

No matter how far we live from family members, and no matter how little we may, perhaps, share in common with them, we still care about and embrace family because we share history and tradition – a common story.

And so it is with Arizona: no matter how far apart we live in this vast state we call Arizona, and no matter how little it may seem we have in common with our fellow Arizonans, we do share a common history and a common story. Will we come to embrace it, commit to it and make it truly our own?

We make a place healthy and vibrant when we make connections between one another, cast off prior domiciles and cynicisms to embrace responsibility for it. That is what it means to "Call Arizona Home."

We Arizonans came here or stay here because we are a hopeful, out-ward-looking people. The pioneers before us left behind a tradition of possibility and of unlimited potential. Whether they came to dig, to plant, to prospect, or to invest, they embraced Arizona's brand of freedom with heart and soul. They were the Spanish explorers and the Hispanic laborers; the Eastern capitalists and the solo entrepreneurs; the small farmers and the developers of new self-contained communities. Our shared tradition is optimism about the future, and we welcome its arrival.

We Arizonans are forgiving. Throughout our history we have embraced those seeking second chances. George Warren lost his stake to the rich Bisbee mine in a footrace and died broke, only to be resurrected as the pictorial image in the Arizona State Seal. And, we are home to countless individuals who met failure elsewhere and who made it here.

We are the original opportunity society.

It could be said, perhaps, that we Arizonans celebrate family even more than other Americans. We move here because it is a uniquely attractive place to raise a family. And we are singularly blessed by the deep family traditions of the Mexican culture and of the Latter-day Saints. How many of us followed other family members here?

While we Arizonans are mostly urban in fact, we are intuitively westerners in attitude. The West was the last to be settled, in part because it was harsher and required more grit and determination to survive. While the many amenities of our large cities make this less so today, it remains true in the rest of the state where jobs are scarce, conveniences lacking and conditions often difficult. But urban and rural alike, we embrace open spaces, celebrate the wild and still untamed, and are motivated by the opportunity to make something new. We live in the West because we see and embrace possibilities as vast as the scenery.

And as we go about enjoying the unique western freedom to fulfill our own separate lives, what are we to make of Arizona?

What obligation do we owe this place that sustains us?

Ten years ago I had the honor of greeting and hosting Pope John Paul II on his visit to Baltimore. In his speech he said: "The basic question of a democratic society is, 'How ought we to live together?'" By way of suggesting an answer he later said, "Genuine freedom is the right to do what you ought, not what you like."

Freedom is both the right to do things and the right to be protected from others. It is the right to take control of governance as well as to be protected from government. Our western tradition all too often celebrates the freedom "from" things, and not the exercise of the freedom "to" embrace the responsibility of governance. We live apart – whether on the open plains of Safford or Kingman or in the confines of our walled patios in Phoenix. We were drawn here by, and often retain, many of the individualist habits that forged the West. And we rail against the regulatory bureaucracies that seem to interfere with our sense of prerogative.

In his book "Democracy in America," Alexis de Tocqueville saw American individualism as its most unique and defining characteristic. He saw it as the engine of our creativity and economic growth. But he also forewarned that if it was not countered by a civic society and a culture of the common good, excessive individualism would be our undoing.

America – and Arizona in particular – is a place of migrants and movers. Our heroes are the wanderers and adventurers, the explorers, the restless cowboys and those who endlessly pursued a better opportunity. Home has always been the place you came from, and the Promised Land the next place you are going.

But, in fact, both are right under our feet.

When we cease to be migrants and become inhabitants we begin to pay more heed and respect to where we are. When we commit to staying, we become stewards. That's what it means to "inhabit." In his book

"Communities and the Politics of Place", former Mayor of Missoula Dan Kemmis writes, "To inhabit a place is to dwell there in a practiced way, in a way which relies on certain regular, trusted habits of behavior."

To inhabit Arizona and fully make it our home we must follow the western tradition of tolerance, trust, and cooperation. We must recognize and renew another western tradition – that of interdependency.

So much of western life, particularly our politics is individualistic, antagonistic and bitter. In modern times this manifests in nasty private property disputes, debates over gun ownership and use, and the growth of cults and other anti-social, separatist lifestyles. (The west, after all, provided refuge for the Unibomber, Nazi skin-heads in Idaho, and polygamists in Utah and Arizona). Antagonisms are an unfortunate part of our western history, with race (Kit Carson's Indian wars are legendary), profit (Bisbee copper miners were physically deported by the mining companies), land disputes (the famed Pleasant Valley War that resulted in families killing families) and religion (the Mountain Meadow massacre that stemmed from religious hatred).

In modern times the disputes pit developers against environmentalists, labor against business, and ever-still ranchers, loggers and farmers against federal regulators. In many instances today's bitter divisions are still over race, profit, land and religion. Each dispute represents a genuine belief that the way of life promised by Arizona is being threatened by those with a different opinion, a different lifestyle or by those in government attempting to balance outside interests.

Such mistrust has become a barrier to our democratic capacity to shape the conditions of our shared existence in this place we call home.

Rarely in public debates, town halls, or letters to the editor do we hear expressions of that mutual stake we have in each other's lives – and of our ultimate interdependency. Instead, they are dominated by "to each his own," or "what's in it for me." Worse, they become the forums for those who engage in personal attack.

In his book "Habits of the Heart," Richard Bellah suggests that individuality in America is like a first language. It is the language we all use unless there are sufficiently compelling reasons to learn a second language – the language of cooperation. As any second language, cooperation does not flourish naturally or automatically; it requires practice, nurturing and good faith. It also requires its practitioners to be place-focused and community-focused. When done well, cooperation is also habit-forming. Once tried, and found successful, good things result.

It is how the West was settled. People knew they could count on one another. Survival depended on the bonds of trust and reliance. This experience has played out in countless ways and places in contemporary times. That is what many of the voices cited in this book have demonstrated.

Sedona has battled the highly individualistic streak inherent in its new-agers and part-time residents to build a new community consensus on the highly controversial Route 179 that cuts through town. However, there remains a deep undercurrent of division over future growth.

Casa Grande forged bonds of trust within its enormously diverse community in making a commitment to create and build a State of the Art Boys and Girls Club, of which they are now rightfully proud. The tools of community-building can presently be used to focus on the rapidly changing demographics of its incoming growth and the potential for badly needed higher paying jobs.

Tucson has drawn on its singular synergy of climate and a university strong in the biosciences to come together around an economic development strategy that could make it a national leader in biomedical sciences. Unfortunately the enormous challenges of an increasingly dysfunctional transportation grid will require another level of leadership and consensus to cure.

Kingman, Lake Havasu City and Bullhead City have demonstrated their ability to work together to build a regional strategy for growth – yet they must continually beat back their competitive tendencies to sustain it.

The gaming Indian tribes have been able to enter into prosperous long-term contracts with the state and with each other. But the partnership is fragile due to a history of mistrust and betrayal.

Sierra Vista has forged an exemplary partnership with Fort Huachuca that has made the base a shared asset for the broader community.

Phoenix has begun to understand that in a mobile, knowledge-based economy, ideas move with the people who have them – and that these people seek communities that are authentic, cherish their history and celebrate a sense of place. This is now happening in downtown Phoenix.

While Prescott has built all the necessary assets to transition from a sleepy "Mayberry town" into a vibrant domicile of new economy workers and the comfortably mobile, it must decide if that is its desired destiny.

The politics of cooperation and trust are occurring with increasing frequency throughout the West as well as throughout our state in communities where citizens put their "place" first and their self-interest second. This is, in a word, "citizenship." It is the assumption of responsibility and the acceptance of inter-dependency.

Sadly, westerners too often see good governance as a commodity to be purchased with tax dollars, but divorced from their own individual lives and aspirations. Yet it is precisely when we withdraw from the field of engaged and responsible citizenship that we surrender to the whims of the greediest or the most powerful among us. We have been there before. We have learned that well-expressed public opinion can trump power and money.

Only a more engaged citizenship can save our politics and strengthen our communities. Communities work – as evidenced by the stories in this book – when people see the connection between their own well-being and the common good, and when there is a shared appreciation for the place being inhabited. To do that, Arizonians must seek a balance of autonomy and community, liberty and common good, individual rights and social responsibility.

Building community and building democracy stem from the same root – the responsibility assumed by each citizen. After voting on the Constitution of the United States, Ben Franklin was asked whether he had created a democracy or a monarchy. He responded, "A democracy, if you can keep it."

How do we keep our communities special in Arizona?

Spiritualists believe that a precondition of personal growth is the need to be "centered." This requires finding a balance in life that is rooted in a mature and an honest sense of who one is. So too with our communities and politics. We will grow healthier and more vibrant communities only when we have a sense – together – of who we are. And that is the power of the stories in this book. By fully inhabiting our "place," the more likely we are to find trust in each other, deeper meaning in our lives, and the means of growing our communities in a spirit of cooperation.

The word "centered" has a double meaning. The hope for community growth lies both in the individual and in finding the political center as well. In the process of self-determining community work, and the participation of an ever-larger group of engaged citizens, it is inevitable that a dialogue of mutual respect will be drawn to the political center where people can find agreement and trust.

We know that we find common ground more often when we move to higher ground.

Along this path, we learn that people's opinions change depending on their personal experiences. Respectful civil dialogue expands the breadth of human understanding and, as a result, enables trust to develop. When we allow debate over public policy – whether water law, education reform, or zoning issues – to be exclusively shaped by technical or statistical considerations, we ignore the more personal and human experiences.

Almost every person interviewed for this book expressed the hope of building the community they love into one that was more vibrant, open, generous, compassionate, tolerant, and just: a place where people are spiritually alive, ecologically and ethically sensitive, loving and caring toward each other. Most recognized the need for trust and cooperation to accomplish it.

There are a myriad of ways that trust and cooperation can grow in Arizona. Political leaders can lower their voices, and seek long-term consensus rather than short-term political advantage. Every form of political action today, from fundraising to media, rewards divisive and confrontational politics. Only mutual respect and the rewards of conscience can reverse the slide we are slipping down.

Business leaders can construct cultural bridges that help to lift the level of tolerance and acceptance within our communities through hiring practices that promote diversity – both on the manufacturing floor, and in the boardroom.

Developers can review open space as enhancing value – and as a legacy opportunity. They can build and develop in ways that promote natural desert landscape, that honor native and Mexican traditions in design and architecture, and in ways that nurture neighborhoods and community.

Environmentalists can come to accept that jobs and well-managed growth are worth making appropriate trade-offs for, and that those who profit from growth are not necessarily "greedy" or insensitive.

Farmers can take every reasonable step to reduce water draw, including crop selection, just as cattlemen can protect the land for sustained grazing by rotating pastures. And the public should support them when they do.

The lumbermen can make long-term investments in forest health by converting their take to smaller diameter trees. And the public should support them when they do.

Seniors can accept the truth that someone else paid for their education, and that they in turn should accept their responsibility to educate the next generation.

Anglos can learn from Native American and Mexican traditions, and all of us can grow to appreciate that diversity makes us stronger and life richer.

Neighbors can cross the street and meet one another in urban as well as in rural settings. We have gone from keeping up with the Jones' to not knowing the Jones'. Phoenix Mayor Phil Gordon is right; the best tool of community is a front porch bench.

It means that Phoenicians will have to lower their patio walls a little bit.

Tucsonans will have to accept growth and its changes, but be demanding about its form and texture in order to preserve their unique heritage.

Residents of Southern Arizona will have to fully embrace the desert that is their home, conserve water accordingly and celebrate the beauty for what it already is.

The growing towns of Prescott, Lake Havasu City, Cottonwood, Sierra Vista and others must plan for the inevitable, and draw upon every part of their communities to reach consensus on how that growth should occur consistent with those towns' history and place. And in the rush to growth they must make extra efforts to preserve that which is historic, or which stimulates human gathering and interaction.

Rural Arizonians will have to more fully embrace the unique heritage of their respective towns, and creatively leverage it into a strategy for tourism, business growth and jobs.

It means that all of us can tread a little more lightly on the land, stay on the trail, smell and listen to the subtlety that is the desert, conserve water, plant less grass, walk and speak a little more softly, and honor the wonderment of this extraordinary place.

The core tenets of this new Arizona are these: Assume responsibility for others, and for the place we inhabit. Be reasonable. Treat the land, the places we live and the people we live among, with respect. Value what we have.

The politics of cooperation and respect and the building of communities based upon those principals are made difficult by many of realities of our world. In "Staying Put," Scott Russell Sanders notes that "our economy rewards competition rather than cooperation, aggression rather than compassion, greed rather than generosity, haste rather than care. Our job culture separates home from work, demands longer hours from employers and punishes those who raise children. The market is brilliant at making money and stupid at making society."

So it is for us to do.

We can start by recognizing that as a new and optimistic state and by virtue of our open attitude and our open space, we have been given a unique chance to try new things and to get it right.

Arizonans have the chance to build new communities that nurture family and inter-connectedness.

Arizonans have the chance to build upon our cultural diversity to show the nation and the world how to get along.

Arizonans have the chance to build new schools that give our children both the roots and the wings to succeed in an ever more competitive world. And universities that create excellence both in the classroom and in the ideas it exports.

Arizonans have the chance to use our open space to assure that the desert is celebrated and that we are at one with, and respectful of, our place.

Arizonans have the chance to create new business and industry, to innovate, to be a competitor in the new global economy.

Arizonans have a chance to build support systems for the most vulnerable among us that shows compassion and tolerance that are the hallmarks of both the new – and old west.

We have a chance – God given and man made – to build a community worthy of this special place we call Arizona.

Sociologist Benjamin Barber wrote in his book "Strong Democracy," 'Through history, democracies have eroded gradually from within, consumed unprotestingly by a complacency in the guise of privatization, by arrogance in the guise of empire, by irresponsibly in the guise of individualism, by selfishness in the guise of rights, by passivity in the guise of deference to experts, by greed in the guise of productivity.'

We must embrace a different kind of community that counters these tendencies with our own commitment to interdependency.

In Arizona the politics of interdependency recognizes the stakes we share in both economic growth and economic justice.

The politics of interdependency recognizes the economic imperative of quality development and the environmental imperative of preserving the open spaces that brought us here.

And the politics of interdependency recognizes that our states heritage lies – and must be sustained – in the towns and on the open land that surrounds our urban areas, but that the urban engines vitality is also the fuel for state-wide prosperity.

The politics of interdependency requires a personal ethic of moral responsibility, a commitment to justice and reconciliation, an economic approach governed by the ethics of community and sustainability, a covenant with the earth, a reminder of shared values that calls forth the very best in us and a renewal of citizen politics to fashion a new political future.

The politics of interdependency recognizes that the more connected people are with each other, the happier they are. Moreover, the more that people are able to self-determine the conditions of their existence and the futures of their communities the healthier they will be. Those who contribute get rewarded, and those who benefit give something back.

The politics of interdependency requires citizenship that embraces the stewardship of our land, water, the fabric of our society, the quality of its health, the education of its citizens, the nurturing of our families, the importance of our religious traditions and the endurance of our democracy.

Interdependency is a tradition as old as the farm barn raisings and Papago canal building of Arizona's earliest days, and is as essential to our survival now as then. Arizona is more than millions of individuals. It is a community of communities. We are all in it together.

"We're beginning to understand that there is nobody else," wrote Dan Kemmis. "That there is nobody but us to take care of the places that we care most about."

And that has always been true. It is a story as old as the West.

"One cannot be pessimistic about the west. This is the native home of hope." Western naturalist and essayist Wallace Stegner wrote in his book "The Sound of Mountain Water." 'When it fully learns that cooperation, not rugged individualism, is the quality that most characterizes and preserves it, then it will have achieved itself and outlived its origins. Then it has a chance to create a society to match its scenery.'

One state – one community – one home at a time.

ABOUT THE AUTHORS

Fred DuVal has called Arizona home since 1964 and has resided in Tucson, Flagstaff and Phoenix. He is a veteran of national and state politics, having served in senior positions in the White House, the U.S. State Department and in the Arizona Governors office. He has published extensively in Arizona newspapers, and has been a commentator on over a hundred television stations and newspapers. He has also been a guest lecturer on many college campuses around the country, and taught a course at Northern Arizona University in 2003. Appointed by Governor Napolitano for the State Commerce Board, he chairs the states planning for a 10 year economic plan. He lives with his wife Jennifer and son Will. And on most mornings he can be found on his favored Circumference Trail at Piestewa Peak.

Lisa Schnebly Heidinger is a native Arizonan whose written works all focus on the Grand Canyon State. Great-granddaughter of Arizona pioneer Sedona Schnebly, she savors traveling the state to connect to all its idiosyncratic charms. A journalist for 25 years, she has reported on everything from drug tunnels to polygamists for television, radio, newspaper and magazine. Her first book, "Tucson, The Old Pueblo," captures her birthplace; the second, a chldren's book, "The Three Sedonas" won Arizona Publishers Association's highest award; then "Chief Yellowhorse Lives On!" is a collection of essays encompassing the best Arizona has to offer. Some of her favorite places in the state are the Schnebly Hill Road overlook, the Vermillion Cliffs, Prescott's Courthouse Square, and the Arizona Inn Library.

ARIZONA'S SEDONA RED ROCKS